NINETEENTH-CENTURY EXPLORERS

FROM LEWIS AND CLARK
TO DAVID LIVINGSTONE

NINETEENTH-CENTURY EXPLORERS

FROM LEWIS AND CLARK TO DAVID LIVINGSTONE

EDITED BY KENNETH PLETCHER, SENIOR EDITOR, GEOGRAPHY

Britannica
Educational Publishing

IN ASSOCIATION WITH

ROSEN
EDUCATIONAL SERVICES

Published in 2014 by Britannica Educational Publishing
(a trademark of Encyclopædia Britannica, Inc.) in association with Rosen Educational Services, LLC
29 East 21st Street, New York, NY 10010.

First Edition

Britannica Educational Publishing
J.E. Luebering: Director, Core Reference Group
Adam Augustyn: Assistant Manager, Core Reference Group
Marilyn L. Barton: Senior Coordinator, Production Control
Steven Bosco: Director, Editorial Technologies
Lisa S. Braucher: Senior Producer and Data Editor
Yvette Charboneau: Senior Copy Editor
Kathy Nakamura: Manager, Media Acquisition
Kenneth Pletcher: Senior Editor, Geography

Rosen Educational Services
Hope Lourie Killcoyne: Executive Editor
Nelson Sá: Art Director
Cindy Reiman: Photography Manager
Brian Garvey: Designer, Cover Design
Introduction by Kenneth Pletcher

Library of Congress Cataloging-in-Publication Data

Nineteenth-century explorers: from Lewis and Clark to David Livingstone/edited by:
Kenneth Pletcher.—First edition.
    pages cm.—(The Britannica Guide to Explorers and Adventurers)
"In association with Britannica Educational Publishing, Rosen Educational Services."
Includes bibliographical references and index.
ISBN 978-1-62275-021-4 (library binding)
1. Explorers—Biography—Juvenile literature. I. Pletcher, Kenneth.
G200.N56 2014
910.92'2—dc23
                                                    2013000704

Manufactured in the United States of America

On the cover: Lewis and Clark's permanent exploring party—known as the Corps of
Discovery—consisted of about 30 men, most of whom were soldiers. This 2004 painting
depicts their ship embarking on May 21, 1804 from the Missouri River town of St. Charles
(just northwest of St. Louis) for what was to be a momentous journey. *Lewis and Clark, 1804*
© *Missouri Bankers Association*

Cover, p. 3 (ornamental graphic) iStockphoto.com/Angelgild; interior pages (scroll) iStock-
photo.com/U.P. Images; interior pages (background texture) iStockphoto.com/Peter Zelei;
pp. viii – xv, 175 (additional background texture) iStockphoto.com Hadel Productions

CONTENTS

12

21

39

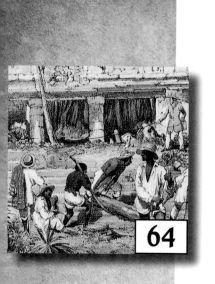

64

84

96

150

165

171

INTRODUCTION

The turn of the 19th century can be said to mark the start of the modern world. The Industrial Revolution, which had begun in Britain in the 1760s, spread to Europe and North America in the early 1800s, helping to set in motion the transformation of those societies from rural and agrarian to urban and industrial—a process still at work today in areas such as China and Southeast Asia. Expanding industrialization required more sources of raw materials and more outlets for manufactured goods, and one of the hallmark themes of the 19th century was the quest by industrializing societies to secure those sources and outlets. As they had in previous centuries, explorers and adventurers played a vital role in this process of expansion into the wider world. *Nineteenth-Century Exploration: From Lewis and Clark to David Livingstone* surveys a broad range of those intrepid and fascinating individuals who, often at great peril, continued and significantly expanded the scope of their famous and lesser-known predecessors.

The result of many of these ventures was colonization or the enlargement of overseas empires, but another, perhaps ultimately more important outcome, was the rise of exploration for scientific discovery and enlightenment. To be sure, explorers had made keen scientific observations in the 18th century, notably during the voyages of James Cook. In the first years of the new century, however, a wholly new breed of explorer emerged whose focus was on observing, collecting, and classifying the overwhelmingly vast wealth of mineral, plant, animal, ethnological, and archaeological wonders of the wider world that had been opened up to them by the explorers and adventurers who had preceded them. Leading the way was the German naturalist Alexander von Humboldt, who undertook detailed scientific work in South America—notably in the Andes Mountains—in the first years of the 1800s.

At almost the same time that Humboldt was wandering far to the south, two Americans, Meriwether Lewis and William Clark, were leading an extraordinary journey in its own right into the largely unknown lands west

Page 26.

Captains Lewis & Clark holding a Council with the Indians

The Lewis and Clark Expedition greets a group of Native Americans, in an engraving by Patrick Gass, one of the members of the expedition. Yale Collection of Western Americana, Beinecke Rare Book and Manuscript Library of the Mississippi River that had just been acquired by a young United States. While it is true that a primary goal of their expedition was to proclaim U.S. sovereignty over these vast regions, the two explorers were also charged by President Thomas Jefferson with observing and recording the new lands, plants, animals, and peoples encountered. The great quantity of specimens brought back, as well as the detailed journals of Lewis, Clark, and other members of the endeavour, became the cornerstone for all future exploration of the American West. Notable among those explorers were Zebulon Montgomery Pike, who encountered the Front Range of the Colorado Rocky Mountains (and for whom Pikes Peak is named); and John C. Frémont, whose activities in the West were instrumental in opening up California and the Pacific Northwest to settlement.

At roughly the same time that Frémont was undertaking his early Western expeditions, the English naturalist Charles Darwin was engaged in his round-the-world journey in 1836–39 aboard the HMS *Beagle*. Darwin, following in the footsteps of Humboldt, was serving as ship's scientist on the voyage, and his observations of finches and other creatures in the remote Galapagos Islands would later prove to be the seeds for his 1859 *On the Origin of Species*, the scientific work that laid the groundwork for the theory of evolution. Two of his contemporaries and friends, Sir Joseph Dalton Hooker and Alfred Russel Wallace, each undertook extensive scientific expeditions that brought back to England enormous collections of plant and animal specimens. Among Wallace's collaborators was the British entomologist Henry Walter Bates, who, in his 11-year exploration of the Amazon Basin in South America, collected thousands of insects and other creatures.

Meanwhile, at around the time that Darwin was returning from his voyage, the American traveler John Lloyd Stephens and English archaeologist Frederick Catherwood were venturing into the Central American jungle. There they discovered the ruins of the lost Mayan civilization and thus inaugurated archaeological study in Middle America. A couple of decades later, the German archaeologist Heinrich Schliemann undertook the first of his expeditions that would discover the ancient city of Troy and other sites that would give rise to the study of ancient Greece.

By the start of the 19th century, the British had established several colonies along Australia's coastlines, but the continent's vast, largely arid interior—the ancient home of Australian Aboriginal peoples—was virtually unknown to Europeans. Beginning with pioneering explorations of New South Wales by George William Evans, John Oxley, and W.C. Wentworth, Europeans began pushing ever deeper into what is now known as the outback. Notable expeditions were undertaken by Charles Sturt, Sir Thomas Livingstone Mitchell, and Hamilton Hume, whose reports soon led to settlement in the regions explored. Later adventurers included the German emigrant Ludwig Leichhardt, Edward John Eyre, and Irish emigrant Robert O'Hara Burke—the latter having led an ill-fated first attempt to cross Australia from south to north.

The interior of Africa, like that of Australia, remained largely a blank slate to Europeans in 1800, but there was great interest in penetrating into the deepest reaches of the continent. Exploration early in the century was focused largely on the somewhat more accessible northern and western regions and included that of the Swiss-born Johann Ludwig Burckhardt, in North Africa and Egypt; the Scottish adventurer Hugh Clapperton, in what is now northern Nigeria; and Alexander Gordon Laing, the first European known to have visited Timbuktu (1826) in what is now northern Mali. Laing died just after leaving the city, but two years later the French adventurer René-Auguste Caillé reached it, survived the return trip, and wrote a popular three-volume account of his journey.

The great objectives for explorers of Africa, however, were its "heart of darkness," the daunting unknown equatorial region centred on the Congo River; and the elusive source of the Nile River in eastern Africa. The desire to open up the continental interior drew men who were to become some of the world's most celebrated and renowned explorers. The Scottish missionary David Livingstone undertook extraordinarily arduous expeditions throughout southern Africa, and his adventures became legendary when, while he was searching for the Nile's source, he was "rescued" by Sir Henry Morton Stanley in 1871. Stanley, after his encounter with Livingstone, went on his own quest for the Nile source but instead found himself within the vast and remote basin of the Congo River, which he explored extensively. The source of the Nile—the great prize that seemed so impossible to attain—spurred the remarkable and intrepid Sir Richard Burton and a determined John Hanning Speke to pursue the quest, both together and separately. Speke reached Lake Victoria in 1858. His claim that this was the source so many had been seeking was initially rejected by Burton—initiating a bitter feud between the two—but ultimately was universally accepted.

The last great frontiers on the planet were the two polar regions. Europeans had been trying for decades to find the legendary Northwest Passage sea route north of

North America that would link the Atlantic and Pacific oceans. Sir John Ross undertook two expeditions (1818 and 1829–33) that pushed farther than anyone else had gone into the Canadian Arctic. He was followed in 1845 by Sir John Franklin, who undertook the most ambitious expedition up to that time. His disappearance in the Arctic came as a great shock to Britain and precipitated numerous rescue attempts over more than a dozen years. Sir Robert McClure, who led one of the Franklin rescue missions, finally completed the first journey through the passage in 1854, although a portion of it was by sledge rather than by sea. The Northeast Passage, the sea route north of the Eurasian landmass, was finally traversed for the first time by the Swedish explorer Baron Adolf Erik Nordenskiöld in 1878–79. Perhaps the greatest Arctic explorer of the century, however, was the Norwegian Fridtjof Nansen, whose three expeditions there included an attempt to reach the North Pole by dogsled in 1895.

Interest in Antarctic exploration was also intense during the first several decades of the 19th century. Three men claimed to have spotted Antarctica in 1820. One of them, Russian explorer Fabian Gottlieb von Bellingshausen, completed a close-in circumnavigation of the continent during his 1819–21 expedition, and another, American Nathaniel Palmer, confirmed that Antarctica was a landmass on his 1819–20 journey. Several other explorers surveyed and charted the coast and coastal features over the next couple of decades— notably French navigator Jules-Sébastien-César Dumont d'Urville (1837–41), American explorer Charles Wilkes (1838–42), and British naval officer Sir James Clark Ross (1839–43)—but it was not until the next century that the continental interior was penetrated.

What drove this fascinating collection of individuals— a disproportionately large number of them British

men—to venture out on such a wide variety of daunting, often physically challenging, and not infrequently
deadly adventures during the 19th century? One reason
certainly was economic. Many started out in the military,
often at an early age, as it was one of the options by which
one from the lower classes could advance in society. This
path had been available for centuries, however. A lasting
legacy of the Enlightenment was the belief that all could
be learned and explained through rational observation
and thought. Although technological advances certainly
made it easier for people to go places that previously had
remained inaccessible, it was this conviction that all was
possible that drove these often larger-than-life individuals to journey into some of the most remote and hostile
places on Earth.

These intrepid souls endured unspeakable hardships
and privations—disease, pestilence, starvation, often
impassable terrain, weather extremes, and the hostil-
ity of local peoples. Still, they would not only venture
once to these places, they would return to them time and
again. Livingstone was gravely ill when Stanley reached
him but once he was well enough he ventured out again
and within a short time was dead. Each person on the
more than two dozen attempts to rescue Franklin's expedition (or, later, to try to determine its fate) certainly
must have been aware that he risked the same fate of
those they sought to find; and, indeed, at one point, one
rescue party managed to save another one that had sailed
out earlier.

As in earlier centuries, women were generally absent
from the exploration scene during the 19th century, other
than being the ones who kept the home fires burning while
their men folk were away on their adventures. Perhaps the
epitome of such a woman was Lady Jane Franklin, whose

active and unflagging pursuit for clues about the fate of her husband continued long after the British government had abandoned the search. A few, such as Livingstone's wife Mary, accompanied their husbands on at least some of their travels. Even more of a standout was Sacajawea, the young Shoshone wife of a man accompanying the Lewis and Clark Expedition, who, for much of the journey, acted as an indispensible interpreter, guide, and liaison between the explorers and Indian peoples the company met along the way. An even smaller number of women actually undertook adventures of their own, such as the remarkable English traveler Mary Henrietta Kingsley, who journeyed extensively through western and equatorial Africa before returning home to lecture and write about the places and people she had encountered.

By the end of the 19th century, most of the habitable world had been visited and explored by a wide range of extraordinary, driven, and intrepid individuals. Tremendous advances had been made in the sciences through the curiosity and detailed observations of a new breed of scientist-explorer. Armed with increasingly sophisticated tools and equipment, these travelers and adventurers had been able to fill in many of the remaining blank spaces in our understanding of the world. They thus set the stage for the remarkable men and women of the 20th and 21st centuries, who undertook a dizzying array of phenomenal feats and achievements that pushed into essentially all of the remaining unexplored corners on Earth—and then began venturing beyond the planet itself and into the "final frontier" of space.

Alexander von Humboldt

(b. September 14, 1769, Berlin, Prussia [now Germany]—d. May 6, 1859, Berlin)

The renowned German naturalist and explorer Friedrich Wilhelm Heinrich Alexander, Freiherr (baron) von Humboldt was a major figure in the classical period of physical geography and biogeography—areas of science now included in the earth sciences and ecology. With his book *Kosmos* he made a valuable contribution to the popularization of science. The Humboldt Current off the west coast of South America was named for him.

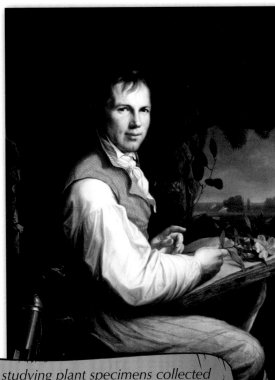

Alexander von Humboldt studying plant specimens collected near the Orinoco River of northern South America. Portrait by Friedrich Georg Weitsch, 1806. SuperStock

EARLY LIFE

Humboldt was the son of an officer in the army of the Prussian king Frederick II the Great. His mother belonged to a family of Huguenots (French Protestants) who had left France after Louis XIV's revocation, in 1685, of religious liberty for Protestants. After his father's death in 1779, he and his brother Wilhelm were raised by their mother, an unemotional woman of strict Calvinist beliefs. They were privately educated; instruction in political history and economics was added to the usual courses in classics, languages, and mathematics, as their mother intended them to be qualified for high public positions. Alexander, a sickly child, at first was a poor student. He was restless, thought of joining the army, and followed his courses only under parental pressure. After futile studies in economics at the University of Frankfurt an der Oder he spent a year in Berlin, where he obtained some training in engineering and suddenly became passionately interested in botany. He began to collect plant specimens in the surroundings of Berlin and learned to classify them. But the poor flora of the province of Brandenburg did not provide much stimulus for an ardent botanist, and Humboldt soon dreamed of journeys to more exotic lands.

A year spent at the University of Göttingen, from 1789 to 1790, finally opened the world of science to him; he became particularly interested in mineralogy and geology and decided to obtain a thorough training in these subjects by joining the School of Mines in Freiberg, Saxony, the first such establishment. Although founded only in 1766, the school had already acquired an international reputation. There, buttressed by a prodigious memory and driven by an unending thirst for knowledge, he began to develop his enormous capacity for work. After a morning spent underground in the mines, he attended classes for five or six hours in the afternoon and in the evening scoured the country for plants.

He left Freiberg in 1792 after two years of intensive study but without taking a degree. A month later he obtained an appointment in the Mining Department of the Prussian government and departed for the remote Fichtel Mountains in the Margraviate of Ansbach-Bayreuth, which had only recently come into the possession of the Prussian kings. There Humboldt came into his own; he traveled untiringly from one mine to the next, reorganizing the partly deserted and totally neglected pits, which produced mainly gold and copper. He supervised all mining activities, invented a safety lamp, and established, with his own funds, a technical school for young miners. Yet he did not intend to make mining his career.

EXPEDITION TO SOUTH AMERICA

The conviction had grown in Humboldt that his real aim in life was scientific exploration, and in 1797 he resigned from his post to acquire with great single-mindedness a thorough knowledge of the systems of geodetic, meteorological, and geomagnetic measurements. The political upheavals caused by the Napoleonic Wars prevented the realization of several scientific expeditions in which Humboldt had been given an opportunity to participate. At last, dispirited by his disappointments but refusing to be deterred from his purpose, he obtained permission from the Spanish government to visit the Spanish colonies in Central and South America. These colonies were then accessible only to Spanish officials and the Roman Catholic mission. Completely shut off from the outside world, they offered enormous possibilities to a scientific explorer. Humboldt's social standing assured him of access to official circles, and in the Spanish prime minister Mariano de Urquijo he found an enlightened man who supported his application to the king for a royal permit. In the summer of 1799 Humboldt set sail from Marseille accompanied by the French botanist Aimé Bonpland, whom he had met in Paris, then the liveliest scientific centre in Europe. The estate he had inherited at the death of his mother enabled Humboldt to finance the expedition entirely out of his own pocket. Humboldt and Bonpland spent five years, from 1799 to 1804, in Central and South America, covering more than 6,000 miles (9,650 km) on foot, on horseback, and in canoes. It was a life of great physical exertion and serious deprivation.

Starting from Caracas (Venezuela), they traveled south through grasslands and scrublands until they reached the banks of the Apure, a tributary of the Orinoco River. They continued their journey on the river by canoe as far as the Orinoco. Following its course and that of the Casiquiare River, they proved that the Casiquiare formed a connection between the vast river systems of the Amazon and the Orinoco. For three months Humboldt and Bonpland moved through dense tropical forests, tormented by clouds of mosquitoes and stifled by the humid heat. Their provisions were soon destroyed by insects and rain; the lack of food finally drove them to subsist on ground-up wild cacao beans and river water. Yet both travelers, buoyed up by the excitement provided by the new and overwhelming impressions, remained healthy and in the best of spirits until their return to civilization, when they succumbed to a severe bout of fever.

After a short stay in Cuba, Humboldt and Bonpland returned to South America for an extensive exploration of the Andes. From Bogotá to Trujillo, Peru, they wandered over the Andean Highlands—following a route now traversed by the Pan-American Highway, in their time a series of steep, rocky, and often very narrow paths. They climbed a number of peaks, including all the volcanoes in the surroundings of Quito, Ecuador; Humboldt's ascent of Chimborazo (20,702 feet [6,310 metres]) to a height of 19,286 feet (5,878 metres), but short of the summit, remained a world mountain-climbing record for nearly 30 years. All of these achievements were carried out without the help of modern mountaineering equipment, without ropes, crampons, or oxygen supplies; hence, Humboldt and Bonpland suffered badly from altitude (or mountain) sickness. But Humboldt turned his discomfort to advantage: he became the first person to ascribe altitude sickness to lack of oxygen (hypoxia) in the rarefied air of great heights. He also studied the oceanic current off the west coast of South America that was originally named for him but is now known as the Peru Current. When the pair arrived, worn and footsore, in Quito, Humboldt, the experienced mountaineer and indefatigable collector of scientific data, had no difficulty in assuming the role of courtier and man of the world when he was received by the viceroy and the leaders of Spanish society.

In the spring of 1803, the two travelers sailed from Guayaquil to Acapulco, Mexico, where they spent the last year of their expedition in a close study of this most developed and highly civilized part of the Spanish colonies. After a short stay in the United States, where Humboldt was received by President Thomas Jefferson, they sailed for France.

Humboldt and Bonpland returned with an immense amount of information. In addition to a vast collection of new plants, there were determinations of longitudes and latitudes, measurements of the components of Earth's geomagnetic field, and daily observations of temperatures and barometric pressure, as well as statistical data on the social and economic conditions of Mexico. Whenever Humboldt had found himself in a centre of commerce in America, he had sent off reports and duplicates of his collections to his brother, Wilhelm, who had become a noted philologist, and to French scientists; unfortunately, the continental blockade then enforced by British ships prevented the greater part of his mail from reaching its destination.

PROFESSIONAL LIFE IN PARIS

The years from 1804 to 1827 Humboldt devoted to publication of the data accumulated on the South American expedition. With the exception of brief visits to Berlin, he lived in Paris during this important period of his life. There he found not only collaborators among the French scientists—the greatest of his time—but engravers for his maps and illustrations and publishers for printing the 30 volumes into which the scientific results of the expedition were distilled. Of great importance were the meteorological data, with an emphasis on mean daily and nightly temperatures, and Humboldt's representation on weather maps of isotherms (lines connecting points with the same mean temperature) and isobars (lines connecting points with the same barometric pressure for a given time or period)—all of which helped lay the foundation for the science of comparative climatology. Even more important were his pioneering studies on the relationship between a region's geography and its flora and fauna, and, above all, the conclusions he drew from his study of the Andean volcanoes concerning the role played by eruptive forces and metamorphosis in the history and ongoing development of Earth's crust. These conclusions disproved once and for all the hypothesis of the so-called Neptunists, who held that the surface of Earth had been totally formed by sedimentation from a liquid state. Lastly, his *Political Essay on the Kingdom of New Spain* contained a wealth of material on the geography and geology of Mexico, including descriptions of its political, social, and economic conditions, and also extensive population statistics. Humboldt's impassioned outcry in this work against the inhumanities of slavery remained unheard, but his descriptions of the Mexican silver mines led to widespread investment of English capital and mining expertise in the mines.

During his years in Paris, Humboldt enjoyed an extraordinarily full life. He had the ability to cultivate deep and long-lasting friendships with well-known scientists, such as the renowned physicist and astronomer François Arago, and to evoke respect and admiration from the common person, an ability that reflected his generosity, humanity, and vision of what science could do. A gregarious person, Humboldt appeared regularly in the salons of Parisian society, where he usually dominated the conversation. He lived simply, in a modest apartment at the top of an old house in the Latin Quarter. His fortune had been seriously depleted by the cost of his expedition and the publication of his books, and for the rest of his life he was often in financial straits. He was, moreover, always willing and eager to assist young scientists at the beginning of their careers. Due to his magnanimity, generosity, and wise judgment, promising students who lacked funds were given the necessary encouragement, financial assistance, and introductions to the scientific community to insure a successful start in life. Such men as the German chemist Justus von Liebig and the Swiss-born zoologist Louis Agassiz owed to Humboldt the means to continue their studies and embark on an academic career. The best proof of his wide interests and affectionate nature lies in his voluminous correspondence: about 8,000 letters remain.

LATER YEARS

The happy years in Paris came to an end in 1827. Humboldt's means by then were almost completely exhausted; unable to maintain his financial independence, he had to return to Berlin, where King Frederick William III impatiently demanded his presence at court. Until a few years before his death, Humboldt served as a tutor to the crown prince (the future Frederick William IV), as a member of the privy council, and as a court chamberlain. He made use of his position to acquaint the young prince and the royal family with scientific methods and the scientific ideas of his time. His enthusiasm for the popularization of science prompted him to give a course on physical geography to the professors and students of all faculties of the University of Berlin, part of which he repeated in a public lecture to an audience of more than 1,000. In the autumn of the same year, 1828, he also organized in Berlin one of the first international scientific conferences. Such large gatherings of possibly liberal-minded people were frowned upon by governments in the wake of the Napoleonic Wars and the attendant rise of democratic expectations, and it is a tribute to Humboldt's adroitness that he was able to overcome the misgivings of official Prussian circles.

In 1829 Humboldt was given the opportunity to visit Russia and Siberia. On the initiative of the Russian minister of finance, Count Yegor Kankrin, he was invited to visit the gold and platinum mines in the Ural Mountains as an adviser to the government on the techniques and organization of mining. But Humboldt had to pledge himself to refrain from commenting on the political situation of the country whose despotism he abhorred. This expedition, lasting only one summer, was very different from the South American journey; the members, Humboldt and two young scientists, were accompanied throughout by an official guard, since they were guests of the tsar. Humboldt and his companions had to endure tiresome receptions at the imperial court and in the homes of provincial governors. They traveled in carriages as far as the Altai Mountains and the Chinese frontier. The resulting geographical, geological, and meteorological observations, especially those regarding the Central Asian regions, were of great importance to the Western world, for Central Asia was then to a large degree unknown territory.

Humboldt passed the last 30 years of his life in Berlin. Once a year he traveled to Paris, where he renewed his contacts with the French scientists, enjoyed daily discussions with his friend Arago, and breathed the cosmopolitan air he so sadly missed in Berlin.

Even before his visit to Russia, he had returned to an investigation of a phenomenon that had aroused his interest in South America: the sudden fluctuations of the Earth's geomagnetic field—the so-called magnetic storms. With the help of assistants, he carried out observations of the movement of a magnetometer in a quiet garden pavilion in Berlin; but it had been clear to him for a number of years that, to discover whether these magnetic storms were of terrestrial or extraterrestrial origin, it would be necessary to set up a worldwide net of magnetic observatories. The German mathematician Carl Friedrich Gauss had already begun to organize simultaneous measurements of the magnetic field by several observatories in Germany, England, and Sweden. In 1836 Humboldt, still interested in the problem, approached the Royal Society in London with the request that it establish an additional series of stations in the British possessions overseas. As a result, the British government provided the means for permanent observatories in Canada, South Africa, Australia, and New Zealand and equipped an Antarctic expedition. With the help of the mass of data produced by this international scientific collaboration, one of the first of its kind, the English geophysicist Sir Edward Sabine later succeeded in correlating the appearance of magnetic storms in the Earth's atmosphere with the periodically changing activity of sunspots, thus proving the extraterrestrial origin of the storms.

During the last 25 years of his life, Humboldt was chiefly occupied with writing *Kosmos*, one of the most ambitious scientific works ever published. Four volumes appeared during his lifetime. Written in a pleasant, literary style, *Kosmos* gives a generally comprehensible account of the structure of the universe as then known, at the same time communicating the scientist's excitement and aesthetic enjoyment at his discoveries. Humboldt had taken immense pains to discipline his inclination to discursiveness, which often gave his writing a certain lack of logical coherence. He was rewarded for his effort by the success of his book, which, within a few years, had been translated into nearly all European languages. While still working on the fifth volume of *Kosmos* with hardly diminished vitality and enthusiasm and with an unimpaired memory, Humboldt died in his 90th year.

DAVID THOMPSON

(b. April 30, 1770, London, England—
d. February 10, 1857, Longeuil, Lower Canada
[now in Quebec, Canada])

David Thompson was an English explorer, geographer, and fur trader in the western parts of what are now Canada and the United States. He was the first European to explore the Columbia River from source to mouth. His maps of western North America served as a basis for all subsequent ones.

Thompson was apprenticed to the Hudson's Bay Company in 1784 and worked as a clerk in northern and western Canada until 1796, when he made an expedition for the company to Lake Athabasca (in present-day northern Alberta and Saskatchewan). He left the company in 1797 to join and become a partner in the rival North West Company and continued to explore and trade on the western plains.

In 1797 Thompson descended a stretch of the Missouri River, and in 1798 he discovered Turtle Lake, one of the headwaters of the Mississippi River. In 1807 he crossed the Rocky Mountains by the Howse Pass and built the first trading post on the Columbia River. Having explored what is now northwestern Montana, Thompson descended the length of the Columbia River in 1811. He then settled in Terrebonne, near Montreal, and drew up maps of the newly explored territory.

Thompson acted as an astronomer and surveyor for the commission that charted the border between Canada and the United States from 1818 to 1826. He conducted other surveys but was not recognized as a geographer until after his death.

WILLIAM CLARK AND MERIWETHER LEWIS

respectively, (b. August 1, 1770, Caroline county, Virginia [U.S.]—d. September 1, 1838, St. Louis, Missouri),

and (b. August 18, 1774, near Charlottesville, Virginia—d. October 11, 1809, near Nashville, Tennessee)

William Clark and Meriwether Lewis were American frontiersmen, military officers, and explorers who shared the leadership of the famous U.S. military expedition of 1804–06 that explored the country's newly acquired

William Clark, portrait by Charles Willson Peale, 1810; in Independence National Historical Park, Philadelphia. Courtesy of the Independence National Historical Park Collection, Philadelphia

uncharted lands of the American Western interior as well as the Pacific Northwest. The company of explorers, formally called the Corps of Discovery, undertook what soon became known as the Lewis and Clark Expedition, a major chapter in the history of American exploration. Clark and Lewis later served in the administration of the country's new lands. Clark played an essential role in the development of the Missouri Territory, and Lewis briefly was governor of Upper Louisiana Territory.

CLARK AND LEWIS BEFORE THE EXPEDITION

Meriwether Lewis, portrait by Charles Willson Peale; in Independence National Historical Park, Philadelphia. Courtesy of the Independence National Historical Park Collection, Philadelphia

Both Clark and Lewis shared similar beginnings. Each was born to an established family in colonial Virginia. Clark's birthplace was some 70 miles (110 km) east of where Lewis was born, and their two birthdays were almost exactly four years apart, Clark being the elder.

The ninth of John and Ann (Rogers) Clark's 10 children, William was born on the family's tobacco plantation in east-central Virginia (roughly equidistant between Fredricksburg and Richmond). In 1785 the family relocated to Louisville, Kentucky, lured there by tales of the Ohio River valley told by William Clark's older brother George Rogers Clark, one of the military heroes of the American Revolution. Like his brother, William Clark was swept up into the American Indian conflicts of the Ohio frontier, joining the militia in 1789 before enlisting in the regular army.

In 1792 U.S. President George Washington commissioned him a lieutenant of infantry. Under General Anthony Wayne, Clark helped build and supply forts along the Ohio River and commanded the Chosen Rifle Company, which participated in the Battle of Fallen Timbers (August 1794), a decisive victory against the Northwest Indian Federation led by Miami Chief Little Turtle. The subsequent treaty signed by Little Turtle one year later secured white settlement in a region that included parts of present-day Ohio, Indiana, Illinois, and Michigan. Clark resigned his commission in 1796 and returned home to regain his health and to manage his aging parents' estate.

Born to William Lewis and Lucy Meriwether, Meriwether grew up on Locust Hill, the family's plantation in Ivy Creek, Virginia—near Monticello, home of the future U.S. president Thomas Jefferson. Lewis's father died while serving in the Continental Army in 1779. His mother then married John Marks and relocated her family to Georgia before being widowed again by 1792. Returning to Virginia, Lewis began managing Locust Hill under his uncle's supervision. He joined the Virginia militia in 1794 to suppress the Whiskey Rebellion (an uprising by farmers in western Pennsylvania who were opposed to a federal whiskey tax). The following year he enlisted in the army at the time of the Northwest Indian War and served for a brief time in Clark's Chosen Rifle Company. Lewis's military career advanced rapidly from ensign (1795) to lieutenant (1799) to captain (1800), and he served as an army recruiter and paymaster. In 1801 President Jefferson asked Lewis to be his personal secretary and aide-de-camp.

LEWIS AND CLARK EXPEDITION

On January 18, 1803, Jefferson sent a secret message to Congress asking for funds to send an officer and a dozen soldiers to explore the Missouri River, make diplomatic contact with Indians, expand the American fur trade, and locate the Northwest Passage (the much-sought-after hypothetical northwestern water route to the Pacific Ocean). The proposed trip took on added significance on May 2, when the United States agreed to the Louisiana Purchase—Napoleon's sale of 828,000 square miles (2,100,000 square km) of French territory to the United States. Jefferson, who had already sponsored several attempts to explore the West, asked Lewis to lead the expedition. Lewis's considerable frontier skills, military service, physical endurance, intellectual prowess, and literary skills made him an excellent choice.

PREPARATION FOR THE EXPEDITION

Lewis traveled to Philadelphia to study celestial navigation, botany, zoology, and medicine with some of the country's brightest scientists and doctors, and he served as the field scientist on the expedition. He also began making preparations, recruiting men, and purchasing equipment and supplies for the expedition. At Harpers Ferry, Virginia (now in West Virginia), he procured weapons, supervised the construction of a 55-foot (17-metre) keelboat, and secured smaller vessels, in addition to designing an iron-framed boat that could be assembled on the journey. Finally, he acquired a Newfoundland dog, named Seaman.

When Jefferson informed Lewis of the numerous commercial, scientific, and diplomatic purposes of the venture, Captain Lewis invited his good friend William Clark to co-command the expedition. Although Clark had been Lewis's superior during the government's battles with the Northwest Indian Federation in the early 1790s, he was officially a lieutenant and second in command to Lewis, because the U.S. secretary of war denied Lewis's request to share the command. The two men, however, chose to address one another as "captain" to mask this bureaucratic distinction from the other members of the expedition. For his part of the preparations, Clark

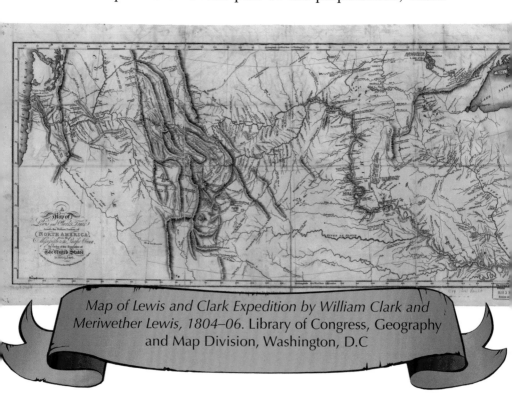

Map of Lewis and Clark Expedition by William Clark and Meriwether Lewis, 1804–06. Library of Congress, Geography and Map Division, Washington, D.C

modified Lewis's keelboat, recruited men in Kentucky and oversaw their training during the winter of 1803–04 at Camp River Dubois in Illinois (on the Mississippi River across from the mouth of the Missouri River), and served as the expedition's principal waterman and cartographer. (Later, his monumental maps of the West, printed in 1810 and 1814, represented the best available until the 1840s.)

THE JOURNEY

Thus, little more than a year following the Louisiana Purchase and after supplies had been floated down the Ohio River and up the Mississippi to the embarkation point at St. Charles (just northwest of St. Louis), Missouri, the Corps of Discovery was ready to depart in the spring of 1804. Their journey was to become a 29-month odyssey that would cover 8,000 miles (13,000 km) and take them through the Great Plains via the Missouri River, into the Rocky Mountains, and across the Continental Divide to the Pacific Ocean and back again. The co-captains advanced the American fur trade by documenting the river systems and fur resources in the West. They met Indian leaders, distributed trade goods, delivered speeches, invited Indian delegations to travel to Washington, and conducted peace, friendship, and trade negotiations. Moreover, they announced the sovereignty of the United States in its newly acquired territory and left calling cards of empire such as medals, flags, and certificates.

The expedition departed on May 14. The entourage, numbering about four dozen men, covered 10 to 20 miles (16 to 32 km) a day—poling, pushing, and pulling their 10-ton keelboat and two pirogues (dugout boats) up the Missouri River. Lewis's iron-framed boat was later assembled and covered with skins near Great Falls (in present-day

Montana), but it had to be abandoned because the seams leaked and there was no pitch to seal them.

The two captains and at least five others kept journals, and the expedition's records constitute a national treasure. President Jefferson had instructed Lewis to make observations of latitude and longitude and to take detailed notes about the soil, climate, animals, plants, and native peoples. Lewis identified 178 plants new to science, including bitterroot, prairie sagebrush, Douglas fir, and ponderosa pine, as well as 122 animals, such as the brown (grizzly) bear, prairie dog, and pronghorn antelope. The scientific names *Philadelphus lewisii* (mock orange), *Lewisia rediva* (bitterroot), and *Clarkia pucella* (pink fairy, or ragged robin) are but three examples of the men's discoveries. The expedition encountered immense animal herds and ate well, consuming one buffalo, two elk, or four deer per day, supplemented by roots, berries, and fish. They named geographic locations for expedition members, peers, loved ones, and even Lewis's dog (Seaman's Creek; now Monture Creek in western Montana). They experienced dysentery, venereal disease, boils, tick bites, and injuries from prickly pears; yet only one man perished over the course of the journey.

Another primary objective involved diplomacy with Native Americans. The expedition held councils with Indians, in which the corps had military parades, handed out peace medals, flags, and gifts, delivered speeches, promised trade, and requested intertribal peace. There also was something of a magic show (magnets, compasses, and Lewis's air gun) and an invitation for Indian representatives to travel to Washington. Most tribes welcomed trading opportunities and provided the expedition with food, knowledge, guides, shelter, and entertainment. The Lakota (encountered in South Dakota), however, already

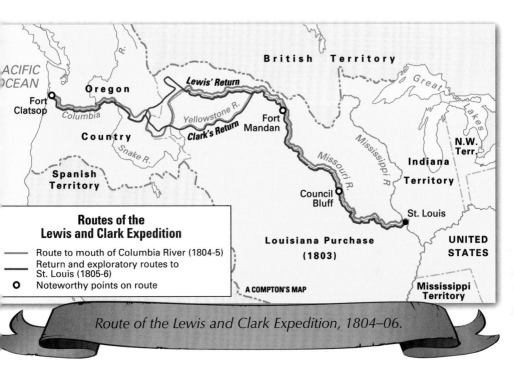

Route of the Lewis and Clark Expedition, 1804–06.

had British commercial ties and did not view American competition favourably, especially because it would make their enemies stronger. Their attempt to prevent the expedition from continuing upstream nearly turned violent, but Chief Black Buffalo's diplomacy defused the situation.

The expedition arrived at the Mandan and Hidatsa villages near present-day Bismarck, North Dakota, and constructed Fort Mandan in which to spend the first winter. The captains prepared maps, artifacts, mineral samples, plant specimens, and papers to send back in the spring. On April 7, 1805, a small crew departed on a St. Louis-bound keelboat laden with boxes of materials for Jefferson that included live magpies and a prairie dog. Meanwhile, the permanent party proceeded up the Missouri in six canoes and two pirogues. It now consisted of 33 people, including soldiers, civilians, Clark's slave York, and two newly hired interpreters—a French Canadian, Toussaint Charbonneau, and his Shoshone wife, Sacagawea, who had given birth to a boy, Jean Baptiste, that February. The departure scene was described by Lewis in his journal:

> *This little fleet altho' not quite so rispectable as those of Columbus or Capt. Cook were still viewed by us with as much pleasure as those deservedly famed adventurers ever beheld theirs...we were now about to penetrate a country at least two thousand miles in width, on which the foot of civillized man had never trodden; the good or evil it had in store for us was for experiment yet to determine, and these little vessells contained every article by which we were to expect to subsist or defend ourselves.*

On June 2, 1805, the expedition party arrived at a fork in the river. Not knowing which waterway was the principal stream, they sent out reconnaissance parties up both forks. Although the evidence was not conclusive, the captains believed the south fork to be the major course while everyone else favoured the north. Lewis named the north fork Maria's River (now Marias River) and instructed the party to continue up the south fork. This choice proved correct when the expedition arrived at the Great Falls almost two weeks later. An 18-mile (29-km) portage around the falls was made even more difficult by broken terrain, prickly pear cactus, hailstorms, and numerous grizzly bears. On July 4, 1805, the party finished the portage and, to celebrate Independence Day, consumed the last of the 120 gallons of alcohol they had brought with them and danced into the night.

Arriving at the Three Forks of the Missouri River (the confluence of the Jefferson, Madison, and Gallatin rivers and the start of the Missouri proper), Sacagawea recognized Beaverhead Rock and informed the others they would soon encounter some Shoshones. Lewis climbed Lemhi Pass, crossing the Continental Divide, only to have his hope for a single mountain portage dashed by the view of endless mountains stretching before him: "I discovered immence ranges of high mountains still to the West of us with their tops partially covered with snow." Fortunately, in mid-August he met a Shoshone band led by Sacagawea's brother Cameahwait, who provided the expedition with horses. The Shoshone guide Old Toby joined the expedition and led them across the Bitterroot Range. On the crossing, Clark lamented, "I have been wet and as cold

Pompey's Pillar, near Billings, Montana, U.S. Travel Montana

in every part as I ever was in my life, indeed I was at one time fearfull my feet would freeze in the thin mockersons [moccasins] which I wore." Cold and hungry, the expedition finally spilled out of the mountains onto the Weippe Prairie, homeland of the Nez Percé. Upon the recommendation of a respected elderly woman, Watkuweis, the Nez Percé befriended the expedition. After leaving their horses with Chief Twisted Hair, the explorers hollowed out five cottonwood canoes and floated down the Clearwater and Snake rivers, reaching the Columbia River on October 16.

They finally arrived at the Pacific Ocean in mid-November, with Clark recording in his journal, "Ocian in view! O! the joy." Fierce storms delayed their progress for nearly a month. The members conducted a democratic vote on where to spend the winter, York and Sacagawea also casting votes. Near present-day Astoria, Oregon, the corps built Fort Clatsop and endured a wet, miserable winter by journal writing, drying meat, making salt, and traveling to see a beached whale. They hoped to encounter vessels along the Pacific that could transport them home, but, finding none, they did an about-face, planning to return along the Columbia and Missouri rivers. After stealing a Clatsop Indian canoe, they headed up the Columbia on March 23, 1806. They arrived at the Nez Percé villages, gathered up their horses, and waited for the snows to melt.

On July 3, after recrossing the Bitterroots, the expedition divided into several groups to better explore the region and two major tributaries of the Missouri. Several groups floated down to the Great Falls, digging up supplies they had cached on their outward journey. Meanwhile, Clark arrived at the Yellowstone River via Bozeman Pass, the route suggested by Sacagawea. After constructing two canoes, he carved his name and the date in a sandstone outcropping, Pompey's Tower (now Pompey's Pillar), from Pomp, the nickname Clark had given Sacagawea's son. In the meantime, Lewis and three men met eight Blackfeet on July 26 on a tributary of Maria's River near present-day Cut Bank, Montana. A deadly altercation occurred the next morning when the explorers shot two warriors who had stolen their horses and guns. Fleeing on horseback for 24 hours straight, the foursome arrived at the Missouri River to rejoin other members of the expedition who were floating downstream. Farther on, this group reunited with Clark, bid farewell to the Charbonneaus, and continued their downstream float, completing the journey on September 23.

Bronze sculpture of Meriwether Lewis, William Clark, and Sacagawea at Fort Benton, Montana. Travel Montana

AFTERMATH AND ASSESSMENT

The Corps of Discovery met with a grand reception upon its arrival at St. Louis. Congress rewarded them with double pay and public land. The captains each received 1,600 acres (650 hectares), and their men received 320 acres (130 hectares). Some of the expedition stayed in the military, others entered the fur trade, while still others took to farming in the region or returned to the East.

Some have insisted that Lewis and Clark's legacy is insignificant because they were not the first non-Indians to explore the area, did not find an all-water route across the continent, and failed to publish their journals in a timely fashion. Although the first official account appeared in 1814, the two-volume narrative did not contain any of their scientific achievements. Nevertheless, the expedition contributed significant geographic and scientific knowledge of the West, aided the expansion of the fur trade, and accomplished a major objective in strengthening U.S. claims to the Pacific.

No American exploration looms larger in U.S. history. The Lewis and Clark Expedition has been commemorated with stamps, monuments, and trails and has had numerous places named for it. St. Louis hosted the 1904 World's Fair during the expedition's centennial, and Portland, Oregon, sponsored the 1905 Lewis and Clark Exposition. In 1978 Congress established the 3,700-mile (6,000-km) Lewis and Clark National Historic Trail. While Lewis and Clark had a great interest in documenting Indian cultures, they represented a government whose policies can now be seen to have fostered dispossession and cultural genocide. This dichotomy was on display during the event's bicentennial, commemorated by two years of special events across the expedition route.

CLARK AND LEWIS AFTER THE EXPEDITION

During the expedition, William Clark had gained an appreciation for the tremendous diversity of native cultures and was often more skillful than Lewis in Indian negotiations. He liked Native Americans, and they seemed to like him; Sacagawea and her family spent the majority of their time with Clark. He also formed a lasting friendship with the Nez Percé and may have fathered a son, Daytime Smoker, with the daughter of Chief Red Grizzly Bear.

In 1807 President Jefferson appointed Clark brigadier general of militia for the Louisiana (later Missouri) Territory and a federal Indian agent for western tribes. Clark supported the "factory system," or government trading houses, which sought to put the government rather than individuals at the forefront of trade with Indians. He also oversaw the construction of Fort Osage on the Missouri River and promoted commercial fur trade activities farther abroad, joining Manuel Lisa in the St. Louis Missouri Fur Company in 1809. During the War of 1812, President James Monroe commissioned Clark territorial governor of Missouri, a position he held from 1813 to 1820. In this role Clark protected settlements and conducted the peace-seeking Treaty of Portage des Sioux in 1815. Later he supervised the removal of tribes located within the Missouri and Arkansas territories. Clark attempted to broker amicable relations between the settlers and the Indians, but Missourians viewed him as too sympathetic to Native Americans.

In Missouri's inaugural gubernatorial election following its attainment of statehood in 1821, Alexander McNair defeated Clark. President Monroe appointed Clark superintendent of Indian affairs at St. Louis in 1822. In that capacity Clark exercised jurisdiction over existing western tribes and eastern nations being removed west of the Mississippi River. He expressed sympathy for those uprooted tribes and promoted their interests as he understood them. Nevertheless, he agreed with and implemented the policy of Indian removal, negotiating 37, or one-tenth, of all ratified treaties between American Indians and the United States. Over the course of his career, millions of acres passed from Indian to U.S. ownership by Clark's hand.

Among his duties, Clark issued trading licenses, removed unauthorized persons from Indian country, and confiscated illegal alcohol. He extended patronage to American fur traders, artists, and explorers who, in turn, assisted him in his mission by establishing friendly relations with numerous tribes. Clark and Secretary of War Lewis Cass wrote a report that resulted in the revision of the Trade and Intercourse Acts and the reorganization of the entire Indian Bureau in 1834. Clark was also a patron of the arts, and he supported the establishment of schools, the growth of banks, and the incorporation of cities. He invested in real estate and railroads, maintained one of the first museums in the West, and promoted other economic and cultural endeavours in the St. Louis area.

Clark was a devoted family man and a valued friend. He and his wife, Julia Hancock, had five children. (He named his eldest son Meriwether Lewis.) The year after his wife's death in 1820, Clark married Harriet Kennerly Radford, a widow with three children, and fathered two more sons. A generous man, Clark served as legal guardian for Sacagawea's children, cared for numerous relatives, and offered assistance to religious groups, missionaries, explorers, and travelers. On the other hand, Clark treated his slave York harshly upon their return from the expedition, although he claimed to have eventually freed him.

In 1807 Jefferson appointed his protégé Meriwether Lewis governor of the Territory of Upper Louisiana. Post-expedition endeavours—preparing a three-volume narrative of the expedition for publication, courting women, reporting back to Jefferson on the treason trial of his former vice president Aaron Burr, and attending to family business—delayed Lewis from assuming his post until March 1808. Trying to govern the territory from the East proved impractical, and Lewis's absence empowered the territorial secretary, Frederick Bates, who undermined

Lewis's authority by setting his own regulations on trading and mining licenses and filling positions through favouritism. When Lewis arrived in Missouri, he clashed with Bates over the administration of Indian and territorial affairs, which resulted in an irreparable rift between them.

In 1809 Lewis, age 35, embarked for Washington, D.C., to explain his public expenditures and to clear his name. Leaving the Mississippi River at Chickasaw Bluffs (now Memphis, Tennessee), he set out along the Natchez Trace, stopping for the evening at Grinder's Stand near present-day Hohenwald, Tennessee, about 70 miles (110 km) from Nashville. There on October 11 Lewis died a violent and mysterious death from gunshot wounds to the head and chest; the circumstances have fueled a long-standing debate over whether his death was a suicide or murder. Many scholars believe Lewis took his own life as a result of depression, alcohol abuse, or failing to marry or to publish. Others assert that thieves, opportunists, or political opponents murdered him. Another explanation suggests it may have been accidental. In 1848 Tennessee erected a grave-site marker that in 1925 became Meriwether Lewis National Monument.

Lewis authorized the construction of Fort Madison on the Mississippi River and Fort Osage on the Missouri River. His attention was also demanded by the Osage Indians, who protested treaties and whose land had been encroached upon by emigrant tribes such as the Cherokee. Lewis faced additional pressures from his superiors regarding his infrequent correspondence and his handling of land claims, mining disputes, unlicensed traders, intertribal warfare, and the delayed return of Mandan Chief Sheheke (who had traveled with Lewis to Washington, D.C.) to his village. Secretary of War William Eustis refused to honour some of Lewis's expense vouchers, which destroyed Lewis's credit and sullied his reputation. Nonetheless, he had been successful in publishing territorial laws and supporting St. Louis's inaugural newspaper. In addition, Lewis, a member of the secret society of Freemasons, had helped establish the first Masonic lodge in Missouri.

SIR JOHN ROSS

(b. June 24, 1777, Balsarroch, Wigtownshire, Scotland—d. August 30, 1856, London, England)

The British naval officer John Ross was one of the early explorers of the Arctic. His first two expeditions (1818 and 1829–33) were in search of the Northwest Passage, the hoped-for North American waterway that would link the Atlantic and Pacific oceans.

On his second expedition, to what is now Canada's Northwest Territories, Ross discovered and surveyed Boothia Peninsula, King William Island, and the Gulf of Boothia. During a sledge journey in 1831, his nephew James Clark Ross located the magnetic pole. The following year the party's ship was crushed in the ice. John Ross and his men were rescued by a whaler in the summer of 1833 and returned to England. In 1834 he was knighted. After serving as British consul at Stockholm from 1839 to 1846, in 1850 he undertook a third and unsuccessful voyage to the North American Arctic in an attempt to find the lost expedition led by explorer Sir John Franklin. Ross became a rear admiral in 1851. He published a number of works, including *Narrative of a Second Voyage in Search of a North-West Passage* (1835).

Sir John Ross, c. 1825. Hulton Archive/Getty Images

FABIAN GOTTLIEB VON BELLINGSHAUSEN

(b. August 18 [August 9, Old Style], 1778, Ösel, Estonia, Russian Empire [now Saaremaa, Estonia]—d. January 13 [January 2], 1852, Kronshtadt, Russia)

Fabian Gottlieb von Bellingshausen (Russian: Faddey Faddeyevich Bellinsgauzen) was a Russian explorer who led the second expedition to circumnavigate Antarctica (1819–21) and for whom was named the Bellingshausen Sea, an area of the Antarctic waters. He entered the Russian navy at age 10 and was an admiral and the governor of Kronshtadt at the time of his death.

Commanding the Vostok and the Mirny, sloops of about 500 tons each, on his Antarctic voyage, he discovered Peter I (January 22, 1821) and Alexander I (January 29) islands in the South Sandwich Island group. These were the first sightings of land within the Antarctic Circle, thought at first to be part of the mainland. His account of the voyage was translated into English in 1945.

ZEBULON MONTGOMERY PIKE

(b. January 5, 1779, Lamberton, New Jersey, U.S.—d. April 27, 1813, York, Ontario, Canada)

The U.S. army officer and explorer Zebulon Montgomery Pike led expeditions into the lands of the new Louisiana Purchase (1803) in the first years of the 19th century. Pikes Peak in Colorado was named for him.

In 1805 Pike, then an army lieutenant, led a 20-man exploring party to the headwaters of the Mississippi River with instructions to discover the river's source, negotiate peace treaties with Indian tribes, and assert the legal claim of the United States to the area. Pike traveled 2,000 miles (3,200 km) by boat and on foot from St. Louis, Missouri, to Leech and Sandy lakes, in northern Minnesota. He erroneously identified Leech Lake as the river's source.

In July 1806 Pike was dispatched to the Southwest to explore the Arkansas and Red rivers and to obtain information about the adjacent Spanish territory. Pike established an outpost near the site of present-day Pueblo, Colorado, and then led his party northwest, where they encountered the Front Range of the Rocky Mountains. After trying unsuccessfully to scale the mountain peak later named for Pike, the party proceeded southward to northern New Mexico, where they were apprehended by Spanish officials on the charge of illegal entry into New Mexico. They were escorted across Texas to the Spanish-American border at Natchitoches, Louisiana, where on July 1, 1807, they were released.

Pike's report on Santa Fe, with information noting particularly the military weakness of the capital and the lucrativeness of the overland trade with Mexico, stimulated the expansionist movement into Texas. Pike served in the War of 1812, attaining the rank of brigadier general. He was killed in action during the attack on York, Ontario.

GEORGE WILLIAM EVANS

(b. January 5, 1780, London, England—d.
October 16, 1852, Hobart, Tasmania, Australia)

The English surveyor and explorer George William Evans was notable for his discoveries in the interior of New South Wales, Australia. As an apprentice to an engineer and architect, Evans learned surveying. In 1796 he emigrated to the Cape of Good Hope (South Africa), and, after British forces withdrew from there in 1802, he went to New South Wales as a storekeeper. In 1802–03 he was appointed acting surveyor-general of that colony.

In 1804 Evans discovered and explored the Warragamba River. Discharged in 1805 by Governor Phillip King, Evans farmed land granted him earlier but failed and in 1809 was appointed assistant surveyor at Port Dalrymple. In 1812 he explored overland to Jervis Bay, where he surveyed its shores; as a result the Illawara region was settled. In 1812 he explored the interior of New South Wales and was appointed deputy surveyor of lands in Van Diemen's Land (now Tasmania). In the course of his seven-week 1813 expedition to the interior of New South Wales, he became the first European to make a complete crossing of the Great Dividing Range. In 1815 he explored further, discovering the Lachlan River, which he followed as far as Mandagery Creek.

In 1817 he was second-in-command to the surveyor-general John Oxley in an expedition to trace the Lachlan River and in 1818 in an attempt to trace the Macquarie River to its source. He resumed his job as a deputy surveyor but went with the first party sent to Macquarie Harbour in 1822. He was implicated in charges of corruption against the deputy governor William Sorell and in 1825 resigned his office, took his pension, and returned to London, where he taught art. As an artist, Evans painted scenes set both in settlements and in the bush.

JOHN OXLEY

(b. 1783/85?, near Westow, Yorkshire, England—d. May 26, 1828, Kirkham, Australia)

John Joseph William Molesworth Oxley was a British surveyor-general and explorer who played an important part in the exploration of eastern Australia and who also helped open up Van Diemen's Land (later Tasmania).

Oxley joined the British navy as a midshipman in 1799 and arrived in Australia as a master's mate in 1802. He worked on coastal surveys and in 1805 was put in command of the Buffalo by Governor Philip King, and in 1806 he commanded another ship to Van Diemen's Land. Commissioned a lieutenant in England in 1807, he returned to Sydney, New South Wales (1808), with a land grant of 600 acres (240 hectares), bringing goods as an investment. In 1809 he wrote a report on the settling of Van Diemen's Land and returned to England.

Oxley was appointed surveyor-general of New South Wales, retired from the navy, and returned to Sydney in 1812. He then explored as much territory as he had surveyed in the early years: in 1817 with George Evans in the

Lachlan River region and in 1818 along the Macquarie River, failing to find these rivers' sources but opening up much land for sheepherding. His *Two Expeditions into the Interior of New South Wales* (1820) was the first description of the area and provided the basis for later explorations by Charles Sturt and T.L. Mitchell.

His coastal surveys included the charting of Jervis Bay and Port Macquarie (1819). In 1823, returning from Port Curtis, he explored Moreton Bay and 50 miles (80 km) up the Brisbane River. His reports led to penal settlements at Port Macquarie and Port Curtis.

From his return in 1812, Oxley had business interests; he was an agent for companies and creditors, engaged in cattle raising, and was a breeder of prize sheep; he also served as bank director and agricultural adviser. On his expanded holdings he built his estate at Kirkham in 1815. Oxley was also active in the Bible Society, institutions for orphans, and the Philosophical Society and served as a magistrate and legislator. He died in straitened circumstances.

JOHANN LUDWIG BURCKHARDT

(b. November 24, 1784, Lausanne,
Switzerland—d. October 15, 1817, Cairo, Egypt)

The Swiss-born adventurer and explorer Johann Ludwig Burckhardt (also known as Ibrāhīm Ibn 'abd Allāh) was the first European in modern times to visit the ancient city of Petra and to arrive at the great Egyptian temple at Abu Simbel (or Abū Sunbul).

Johann Ludwig Burckhardt. Apic/Hulton Archive/Getty Images

Burckhardt went to England in 1806 and studied in London and at Cambridge University. In 1809, under the auspices of the Association for Promoting the Discovery of the Interior Parts of Africa, he visited Syria to learn Arabic and to accustom himself to Muslim life. According to instructions from the London association, he was then to journey to the regions south of the Sahara, via Fezzan, now the southwestern sector of Libya. In 1812, en route from Syria to Cairo, he discovered the important archaeological site at Petra, in modern Jordan. Upon his arrival in Cairo he found no immediate prospect for a reliable caravan to Fezzan; hence he decided to travel up the Nile. In so doing he discovered the temple at Abu Simbel, generally thought to be among the most imposing of all rock temples. Next he traveled through Arabia, visiting Mecca. He then returned to Cairo where he died, still waiting for a chance to cross the Sahara.

Burckhardt, who took a Muslim name and often wore Muslim dress, left his large collection of Arabic manuscripts to the University of Cambridge. His writings include *Travels in Nubia* (1819), *Travels in Syria and the Holy Land* (1822), and *Travels in Arabia* (1829).

EDWARD BRANSFIELD

(b. c. 1785—d. 1852)

The English naval officer Edward Bransfield is believed to have been the first to sight the Antarctic mainland and to chart a portion of it.

Master aboard HMS *Andromache* at Valparaiso, Chile, he was appointed to sail the two-masted brig *Williams* in order to chart the recently sighted South Shetland Islands, which lie near the Antarctic Peninsula. Under Bransfield's command, the *Williams* arrived at the South Shetlands in January 1820, landed on King George Island to take formal possession, and coasted past Deception Island. Turning southward into what is now called the Bransfield Straight, he sighted and charted "high mountains, covered with snow," now Mounts Bransfield and Jacquinot on the Antarctic mainland (January 30, 1820). The charts survive in the hydrographic department of the British Admiralty at Taunton, Somerset, England.

DIXON DENHAM

(b. January 1, 1786, London, England—d. May 8, 1828, Freetown, Sierra Leone)

Dixon Denham was a British soldier who became one of the early explorers of western Africa. After serving in the Napoleonic Wars, he volunteered in 1821 to join Walter Oudney and Lieutenant Hugh Clapperton on an official expedition across the Sahara to Bornu (now in northeastern Nigeria), in the Lake Chad basin. After enduring danger and privation, they arrived at Kuka, the capital of Bornu, on February 17, 1823. In December 1823, while Clapperton and Oudney set out on a journey westward, Denham explored the shores of Lake Chad and the lower courses of the Waubé, Chari, and Logone rivers.

Returning to England in 1825, Denham became a celebrity. He was promoted to lieutenant colonel and appointed superintendent of liberated slaves in West Africa in 1827. The next year he was made governor of Sierra Leone, where he died of fever.

SIR JOHN FRANKLIN

(b. April 16, 1786, Spilsby, Lincolnshire,
England—d. June 11, 1847, near King William
Island, British Arctic Islands [now in Nunavut
territory, Canada])

English rear admiral and explorer Sir John Franklin led an ill-fated expedition (1845) in search of the Northwest Passage, a North American Arctic waterway connecting the Atlantic and Pacific oceans. After it was determined that Franklin had been lost, efforts to find him and his crew became one of the major goals of Arctic explorers in the mid-19th century.

Franklin entered the Royal Navy at the age of 14, accompanied Matthew Flinders on his exploratory voyage to Australia (1801–03), and served in the battles of Trafalgar (1805) and New Orleans (1814). He commanded the *Trent* on Captain David Buchan's Arctic expedition of 1818, which sought to reach the North Pole.

From 1819 to 1822 Franklin conducted an overland expedition from the western shore of Hudson Bay to the Arctic Ocean, and he surveyed part of the coast to the east of the Coppermine River in northwestern Canada. After

his return to England he published *Narrative of a Journey to the Shores of the Polar Sea, in the Years 1819, 20, 21 and 22* (1823).

On a second overland expedition to the same region (1825–27), Franklin led a party that explored the North American coast westward from the mouth of the Mackenzie River, in northwestern Canada, to Point Beechey, now in Alaska. A second party followed the coast eastward from the Mackenzie to the Coppermine. These efforts, which added new knowledge of about 1,200 miles (1,932 km) of the northwest rim of the North American coastline, were described in *Narrative of a Second Expedition to the Shores of the Polar Sea, in the Years 1825, 1826, and 1827* (1828). Knighted in 1829, Franklin served as governor of Van Diemen's Land (now Tasmania) from 1836 to 1843.

Franklin's search for the Northwest Passage began on May 19, 1845, when he sailed from England with two ships, the *Erebus* and the *Terror*, carrying 128 officers and men.

Having ascended the Wellington Channel, in the Queen Elizabeth Islands, to latitude 77° N, the *Erebus* and the *Terror* wintered at Beechey Island (1845–46). Returning southward along the western side of Cornwallis Island, they passed through Peel Sound and Franklin Strait. In September 1846 they became trapped in the ice in Victoria Strait, off King William Island (about midway between the Atlantic and Pacific oceans). By April 1848, Franklin and 23 others had perished there. The ships, still gripped by ice, were deserted on April 22, 1848, and the 105 survivors tried to head south across the North American mainland to the Back River, apparently resorting to cannibalism along the way.

The vessels had last been sighted by British whalers north of Baffin Island at the entrance to Lancaster Sound in late July 1845, a couple of months after the voyage began. Two years later, in 1847, when no word had been received, search parties were sent out. For 12 years thereafter, various expeditions sought the explorers, but their fate was unknown until 1859, when a final search mission, sent in 1857 by Franklin's second wife, Lady Jane Franklin, and headed by Captain Francis Leopold McClintock, reached King William Island, south and west of Lancaster Sound. Found were skeletons of the vessels' crews and a written account of the expedition through April 25, 1848.

An old Eskimo woman told McClintock of how the starving men fell down and died as they walked. Franklin himself never proved the existence of the Northwest Passage, but a small party from his expedition may have reached Simpson Strait, which connected with the western coastal waters previously visited by Franklin. Postmortems conducted on the preserved bodies of several crew members suggest that lead poisoning from eating faultily tinned food may have contributed to the mental and physical decline of the expedition.

JAMES WEDDELL

(b. August 24, 1787, Ostend, Austrian
Netherlands [now in the Netherlands]—
d. September 9, 1834, London, England)

The renowned British explorer and seal hunter James Weddell set a record for navigation into the Antarctic region. The Weddell Sea, bordered to the west by the Antarctic Peninsula, is named for him.

Weddell commanded the sealing brig *Jane* on three Antarctic voyages, the success of the first (1819–21) permitting him to buy a share in the vessel. On the second voyage (1821–22) he visited the island of South Georgia, east of the tip of South America, as well as the South Shetland Islands. In February 1822 he visited and named the South Orkney Islands. On his third voyage (1822–24) he surveyed the South Shetlands and the South Orkneys and then sailed southward in search of new land. Aided by unusually open ice conditions, he reached latitude 74°15' S in the sea that was later named for him, exceeding James Cook's record of southernmost exploration by more than three degrees of latitude. He left a record of his exploration in *A Voyage Towards the South Pole* (1825).

HUGH CLAPPERTON

(b. May 18, 1788, Annan, Dumfries,
Scotland—d. April 13, 1827, near Sokoto, Fulani
Empire [now in Nigeria])

The Scottish adventurer Hugh Clapperton became the first European explorer in western Africa to return with a firsthand account of the region now known as northern Nigeria. Following service in the Royal Navy, he joined explorers Dixon Denham and Walter Oudney in a British government expedition that journeyed southward from Tripoli [Libya] across the Sahara. Early in 1823 they became the first Europeans to view Lake Chad and to enter the Sudanese province of Bornu, now in Nigeria. Clapperton traveled to Kano, Katsina, Sokoto, and Zaria, all now in Nigeria, before he and Denham returned to England in June 1825.

Almost immediately Clapperton sailed to the west coast of Africa. In December he left the Bight of Benin for the Niger River with his servant and companion, Richard Lander. They crossed the Niger and traveled via Kano to Sokoto, near which Clapperton died. His *Narrative of*

Travels and Discoveries in Northern and Central Africa in the Years 1822–1823, and 1824 was published in 1828. Lander published *Records of Captain Clapperton's Last Expedition to Africa* in 1830.

BASIL HALL

(b. December 31, 1788, Dunglass, Haddingtonshire, Scotland—d. September 11, 1844, Gosport, Hampshire, England)

The British naval officer and traveler Basil Hall is remembered for noteworthy accounts of his visits to East Asia, Latin America, and the United States.

The son of geologist Sir James Hall, the younger Hall joined the navy in 1802. In 1815 he commanded the escort ship that accompanied William Pitt Amherst (Earl Amherst), the English ambassador to China, who was to present himself to the emperor at Beijing. Hall published a description of his explorations conducted in the course of his mission, *Account of a Voyage of Discovery to the West Coast of Corea, and the Great Loo-Choo Island* (1818). He put to sea for service in South America (1820) and described his experiences in *Extracts from a Journal Written on the Coasts of Chili, Peru and Mexico, in the Years 1820, 1821, 1822,* 2 vol. (1824). After leaving the navy he went to the United States, and upon returning to England he published a work, *Travels in North America in the Years 1827 and 1828,* 3 vol. (1829), that was attacked by an American press sensitive to criticism of America (especially concerning slavery) by Europeans. From 1842 until his death he was confined as a mental patient in Haslar Naval Hospital, Gosport.

SACAGAWEA

(b. *c.* 1788, near the Continental Divide at the present-day Idaho-Montana border [U.S.]— d. December 20, 1812?, Fort Manuel, on the Missouri River, Dakota Territory [near present-day Mobridge, South Dakota])

Sacagawea (also spelled Sacajawea) was a Shoshone Indian woman who, as interpreter, traveled thousands of wilderness miles with the Lewis and Clark Expedition (1804–06), from the Mandan-Hidatsa villages in the Dakotas to the Pacific Northwest.

Separating fact from legend in Sacagawea's life is difficult; historians disagree on the dates of her birth and death and even on her name. In Hidatsa, Sacagawea (pronounced with a hard g) translates into "Bird Woman." Alternatively, Sacajawea means "Boat Launcher" in Shoshone. Others favor Sakakawea. The Lewis and Clark journals generally support the Hidatsa derivation.

A Lemhi Shoshone woman, she was about 12 years old when a Hidatsa raiding party captured her near the Missouri River's headwaters about 1800. Enslaved and taken to their Knife River earth-lodge villages near present-day Bismarck, North Dakota, she was purchased by French Canadian fur trader Toussaint Charbonneau and became

Sacagawea, interpreting Lewis and Clark's intentions to the Chinook Indians. Lewis and Clark were the first to ethnographically describe the Chinook, North American Indians who were famous as traders, with connections stretching as far as the Great Plains. MPI/Archive Photos/ Getty Images

one of his multiple wives about 1804. They resided in one of the Hidatsa villages, Metaharta.

When explorers Meriwether Lewis and William Clark arrived at the Mandan-Hidatsa villages and built

Fort Mandan to spend the winter of 1804–05, they hired Charbonneau as an interpreter to accompany them to the Pacific Ocean. Because he did not speak Sacagawea's language and because the expedition party needed to communicate with the Shoshones to acquire horses to cross the mountains, the explorers agreed that the pregnant Sacagawea should also accompany them. On February 11, 1805, she gave birth to a son, Jean Baptiste.

Departing on April 7, the expedition ascended the Missouri. On May 14, Charbonneau nearly capsized the white pirogue in which Sacagawea was riding. Remaining calm, she retrieved important papers, instruments, books, medicine, and other indispensable valuables that otherwise would have been lost. During the next week Lewis and Clark named a tributary of Montana's Mussellshell River "Sah-ca-gah-weah," or "Bird Woman's River," for her. She proved to be a significant asset in numerous ways: searching for edible plants, making moccasins and clothing, as well as allaying suspicions of approaching Indian tribes through her presence; a woman and child accompanying a party of men indicated peaceful intentions.

By mid-August the expedition encountered a band of Shoshones led by Sacagawea's brother Cameahwait. The reunion of sister and brother had a positive effect on Lewis and Clark's negotiations for the horses and guide that enabled them to cross the Rocky Mountains. Upon arriving at the Pacific coast, she was able to voice her opinion about where the expedition should spend the winter and was granted her request to visit the ocean to see a beached whale. She and Clark were fond of each other and performed numerous acts of kindness for one another, but romance between them occurred only in latter-day fiction.

Sacagawea was not the guide for the expedition, as some have erroneously portrayed her; nonetheless, she recognized landmarks in southwestern Montana and informed

Clark that Bozeman Pass was the best route between the Missouri and Yellowstone rivers on their return journey. On July 25, 1806, Clark named Pompey's Tower (now Pompey's Pillar) on the Yellowstone for her son, whom Clark fondly called his "little dancing boy, Pomp."

The Charbonneau family disengaged from the expedition party upon their return to the Mandan-Hidatsa villages; Charbonneau eventually received a stipend and 320 acres (130 hectares) for his services. Clark wanted to do more for their family, so he offered to assist them and eventually secured Charbonneau a position as an interpreter. The family traveled to St. Louis in 1809 to baptize their son and left him in the care of Clark, who had earlier offered to provide him with an education. Shortly after the birth of a daughter named Lisette, a woman identified only as Charbonneau's wife (but believed to be Sacagawea) died at the end of 1812 at Fort Manuel, near present-day Mobridge, South Dakota. Clark became the legal guardian of Lisette and Jean Baptiste and listed Sacagawea as deceased in a list he compiled in the 1820s. Some biographers and oral traditions contend that it was another of Charbonneau's wives who died in 1812 and that Sacagawea went to live among the Comanches, started another family, rejoined the Shoshones, and died on Wyoming's Wind River Reservation on April 9, 1884. These accounts can likely be attributed to other Shoshone women who shared similar experiences as Sacagawea.

Sacagawea's son, Jean Baptiste, traveled throughout Europe before returning to enter the fur trade. He scouted for explorers and helped guide the Mormon Battalion to California before becoming an alcalde, a hotel clerk, and a gold miner. Lured to the Montana goldfields following the Civil War, he died en route near Danner, Oregon, on May 16, 1866. Little is known of Lisette's whereabouts prior to her death on June 16, 1832; she was buried in the

Old Catholic Cathedral Cemetery in St. Louis. Charbonneau died on August 12, 1843.

Sacagawea has been memorialized with statues, monuments, stamps, and place-names. In 2000 her likeness appeared on a gold-tinted dollar coin struck by the U.S. Mint. In 2001 U.S. President Bill Clinton granted her a posthumous decoration as an honorary sergeant in the regular army.

WILLIAM SCORESBY

(b. October 5, 1789, Cropton, near Whitby, Yorkshire, England—d. March 21, 1857, Torquay, Devon)

The English explorer, scientist, and clergyman William Scoresby was a pioneer in the scientific study of the Arctic and contributed to the knowledge of terrestrial magnetism.

At the age of 10 Scoresby made his first Arctic whaling voyage aboard his father's ship, the *Resolution*, which he later commanded in 1811. In 1813 he established that the temperature of polar waters is warmer at great depths than at the surface. His *Account of the Arctic Regions with a History and Description of the Northern Whale-Fishery* (1820) contained his own findings as well as those of earlier navigators. His voyage to Greenland in 1822, during which he surveyed 400 miles (650 km) of the east coast, was his last venture into the Arctic. He then began divinity studies at Cambridge and later became a clergyman. His new career did not, however, end his scientific work. In 1848, while crossing the Atlantic Ocean, he made valuable observations on the height of waves. He also voyaged to Australia in 1856 to gather data on Earth's magnetism.

JULES-SÉBASTIEN-CÉSAR DUMONT D'URVILLE

(b. May 23, 1790, Condé-sur-Noireau, France—d. May 8, 1842, near Meudon)

The French navigator Jules-Sébastien César Dumont d'Urville commanded two voyages of exploration to the South Pacific Ocean (1826–29) and the Antarctic region (1837–40), resulting in extensive revisions of existing charts and discovery or redesignation of island groups.

In 1820, while on a charting survey of the eastern Mediterranean Sea, d'Urville helped the French government gain possession of what became one of the best-known Greek sculptures, the *Venus de Milo*, which had been unearthed on the Aegean island of Mílos in that year. In 1822 he served on a voyage around the world and returned to France in 1825. His next mission took him to the South Pacific, where he searched for traces of explorer Jean-François La Pérouse, lost in that region in 1788. On this voyage he charted parts of New Zealand and visited the Fiji and Loyalty islands, New Caledonia, New Guinea, Amboyna, Van Diemen's Land (now Tasmania), the Caroline Islands, and the Celebes. In February 1828 d'Urville sighted wreckage, believed to be from the frigates of La Pérouse, at Vanikoro in the Santa Cruz Islands.

The expedition returned to France on March 25, 1829. The voyage resulted in extensive revision in charts of South Sea waters and redesignation of island groups into Melanesia, Micronesia, Polynesia, and Malaysia. D'Urville also returned with about 1,600 plant specimens, 900 rock samples, and information on the languages of the islands he had visited. Promoted to *capitaine de vaisseau* (captain) in 1829, he conveyed the exiled king Charles X to England in August 1830.

In September 1837 d'Urville set sail from Toulon on a voyage to Antarctica. He hoped to sail beyond the latitude 74°15' S reached by James Weddell in 1823. After surveying in the Straits of Magellan, d'Urville's ships reached the pack ice at latitude 63°29' S, longitude 44°47' W, but they were ill-equipped for ice navigation. Unable to penetrate the pack, they coasted it for 300 miles (480 km) to the east. Heading westward, they visited the South Orkney and the South Shetland islands and discovered Joinville Island and Louis Philippe Land before scurvy forced them to stop at Talcahuano, Chile. After proceeding across the Pacific to the Fiji and Pelew (now Palau) islands, New Guinea, and Borneo, they returned to the Antarctic, hoping to discover the magnetic pole in the unexplored sector between longitude 120° and 160° E. In January 1840 they sighted the Adélie coast, south of Australia, and named it for Mme d'Urville. The expedition reached France late in 1841. The following year d'Urville was killed, with his wife and son, in a railway accident.

Dumont d'Urville's chief works include (with others) *Voyage de la corvette "l'Astrolabe," 1826–1829* (1830–34; "Voyage of the Corvette 'Astrolabe,' 1826–1829"), *Voyage au Pole Sud et dans l'Océanie, 1837–1840* (1841–54; "Voyage to the South Pole and in Oceania, 1837–1840"), and *An Account in Two Volumes of Two Voyages to the South Seas* (1987).

W.C. WENTWORTH

(b. 1790, Norfolk Island, New South Wales
[Australia]—d. March 20, 1872, Wimborne,
Dorset, England)

W.C. (William Charles) Wentworth was the leading Australian political figure during the first half of the 19th century, whose lifelong work for self-government culminated in the New South Wales constitution of 1855.

Wentworth became a public figure in 1813, when his crossing of the Blue Mountains near the coast of New South Wales opened up a vast new area for grazing. His book *A Statistical, Historical, and Political Description of the Colony of New South Wales and Its Dependent Settlements in Van Diemen's Land* (1819) publicized opportunities for colonization and argued for a liberal voting franchise. In 1824 he started a newspaper, the *Australian*, utilizing it and the Australian Patriotic Association, which he headed in 1835, to campaign for representative government.

After 1837 Wentworth sided with the large landowners and others who wanted a property-based franchise. He continued to work for home rule, making possible the Constitution Act of 1842, which provided for the election (rather than appointment) of two-thirds of the Legislative Council in New South Wales, and the constitution of the colony adopted in 1855. In 1853 he made the earliest proposal for federal government in Australia and led the upper house in 1861. He also helped to establish state primary education and the first Australian university, at Sydney, in 1850. He retired to England in 1862.

SIR THOMAS LIVINGSTONE MITCHELL

(b. June 15, 1792, Craigend, Stirlingshire, Scotland—d. October 5, 1855, Sydney, New South Wales [Australia])

Sir Thomas Livingstone Mitchell was the surveyor general of New South Wales who explored and surveyed widely in Australia during the first half of the 19th century.

As a soldier in the Peninsular War in Spain (1811–14), Mitchell worked in topographical intelligence. He became a major in 1826 but was placed on half pay. In 1827 he went to New South Wales as assistant surveyor general to John Oxley at Sydney. He succeeded Oxley in 1828, assuming responsibility for roads and bridges in 1829 and in 1830 sole responsibility for the whole department. By 1830 he had established permanent routes from Sydney to Parramatta and to Liverpool and through the Blue Mountains.

In 1831–32 Mitchell explored between the Castlereagh and Gwydir rivers. In 1835 he traced the Darling River from the point at which Charles Sturt had left off in 1828 to the junction with the Murray River. In 1836 his exploration of land around the Murray led him to call the area Australia Felix (Happy Australia; later, Victoria state). The area was settled rapidly thereafter.

In 1837 Mitchell went on leave to England and wrote *Three Expeditions into Eastern Australia* (1838) and began a campaign for knighthood (granted in 1839). He also published his Peninsular War battle plans in 1840.

Mitchell returned to Australia in 1841 and in 1844 was elected to the legislative council. His fourth expedition (1845–46) sought in vain an overland route to Port Essington, but he surveyed a vast area.

Again on leave in England (1847–48), Mitchell wrote *Journal of an Expedition into the Interior of Tropical Australia* (1848) and *The Australian Geography* (1850), used as a textbook in Australian schools.

ALEXANDER GORDON LAING

(b. December 27, 1793, Edinburgh, Scotland—
d. September 26, 1826, near Timbuktu, Fulani
empire [now Timbuktu, Mali])

The Scottish explorer of western Africa Alexander Gordon Laing was the first European known to have reached the ancient city of Timbuktu.

Serving with the British army in Sierra Leone (1822), Laing was sent among the Mande people of the region by the governor, Charles (later Sir Charles) M'Carthy, to attempt to develop trade in goods and to abolish that in slaves. He also visited the capital of the Susu people, Falaba, now in Sierra Leone. In 1823–24 Laing fought in the war between the British and the Asante empire and returned to England with the news of M'Carthy's death in action.

His next mission was to visit Timbuktu and to explore the Niger River basin. In July 1825 he left the North African coast at Tripoli, Libya, on his journey across the Sahara. He reached Ghadāmis (Ghadames) in northern Fezzan, now in Libya, by September and then entered the vast country of the Tuareg. Before reaching Timbuktu on August 18, 1826, he had to fight for his life and was severely wounded. He left Timbuktu on September 24 and was murdered two days later. The journal of his earlier explorations, *Travels in the Timannee, Kooranko, and Soolima Countries in Western Africa*, was published in 1825.

CHARLES STURT

(b. April 28, 1795, Bengal, India—d. June 16, 1869, Cheltenham, Gloucestershire, England)

Charles Sturt was the Australian explorer whose expedition down the Murrumbidgee and Murray rivers (1829–30) is considered one of the greatest explorations in Australian history. The expedition disclosed extensive areas of land for future development in New South Wales and South Australia.

Educated in England, Sturt entered the British Army at the age of 18 and for the next 13 years saw service in Spain, Canada, France, and Ireland. In 1827 he became military secretary to the governor of New South Wales, Sir Ralph Darling. In 1828–29 Sturt led the first of his major expeditions, tracing the Macquarie, Bogan, and Castlereagh rivers and discovering the Darling River. In his subsequent expedition down the Murrumbidgee, he discovered the Murray River and followed it to its mouth near Adelaide, dealing peaceably with many Aboriginal peoples along the way. Exhausted and nearly blinded because of poor diet and overexertion on his trip, he spent 1832–34 recuperating in England, where he wrote *Two Expeditions into the Interior of Southern Australia, 1828–31* (1833). The book led to the choice of South Australia as the site for a new British settlement.

Sturt returned to Australia in 1834 with a 5,000-acre (2,000-hectare) grant of land and later (1844–46) led an expedition north from Adelaide to the edge of Simpson Desert. Although it discovered no fertile land and was eventually driven back by heat and scurvy, his party was the first to penetrate the centre of the continent. After serving briefly as registrar general and colonial treasurer, he again left Australia for England (1847), where he wrote *Narrative of an Expedition into Central Australia* (1849). He settled in England permanently in 1853. In New South Wales, Sturt National Park, which encompasses some 1,200 square miles (3,100 square km), commemorates his achievements.

ROBERT MOFFAT

(b. December 21, 1795, Ormiston, East Lothian, Scotland—d. August 9, 1883, Leigh, Kent, England)

The Scottish missionary to Africa and Bible translator Robert Moffat was known for his efforts to
improve local living standards in Africa. He was also
the father-in-law of the missionary and explorer David
Livingstone (1813–73).

With little training, Moffat was assigned in 1816 by the
London Missionary Society to go to South Africa. After
spending seven years in several locations that were dis-
rupted by warfare among Zulu tribesmen, he settled at
Kuruman, southeast of the Kalahari (desert). There he
lived for 49 years, building one of the foremost Protestant
missionary communities in Africa. He traveled widely,
and he encountered numerous peoples and mastered
the Tswana language, into which he translated the *Gospel
According to Luke* (1830). Through his influence the number of converts rose rapidly, and by 1857 he had completed
a Tswana translation of the entire Bible. In 1838 he wrote
A Book of Hymns in Chuana (Tswana).

Though criticized by some as paternalistic, he
laboured not only to alter the conduct but also to raise
the standard of living of African peoples by introducing
improved methods of agriculture and irrigation. On his
first meeting with Livingstone, in 1840, Moffat recognized Livingstone's capacities and urged him to come to
Africa, directing him to the region north of the Kalahari.
After the death of his wife, Mary, with whom he shared his
work for half a century, Moffat lived his remaining 13 years
in retirement in England.

Among Moffat's writings are *Missionary Labours and
Scenes in Southern Africa* (1842) and *Rivers of Water in a Dry
Place* (1863).

HAMILTON HUME

(b. June 19, 1797, near Parramatta, New South
Wales, Australia—d. April 19, 1873, Coomer
Cottage, Yass, New South Wales)

Hamilton Hume was a Welsh explorer whose work did
much to open up the Berrima-Bong Bong District
of Australia.

Hume was the eldest son of Andrew Hamilton Hume
(1762–1849), a farmer and a superintendent of convicts.
The son began exploring at the age of 17 with his brother
John and an Aborigine, and extended his range (1814–15).
He traveled with Charles Throsby and James Meehan
(1818), accompanied John Oxley and Meehan to Port Jervis
(1819), and with others discovered the Yass Plains (1822).

Unable to get financial support from the government for an overland expedition to the southern coast of
Australia, Hume accepted that of William Hovell, a sailor
whose inexperience in the bush was compensated by his
skill at navigation. They traversed from Gunning to Corio
Bay (October 1824–January 1825), discovering part of the
Murray River and valuable farming and grazing lands. For
this journey Hume was rewarded by a grant of 500 acres
(200 hectares) on the Crookhaven River.

In 1828 Hume accompanied Charles Sturt on an
expedition that discovered Darling River, but as a result
his health was broken, and he settled on the Yass Plains,
where he was granted 500 acres by Governor Darling.

When in 1853 Hovell visited Geelong, established after his and Hume's 1824–25 exploration, and was celebrated as its discoverer, Hume wrote *A Brief Statement of Facts in Connection with an Overland Journey from Lake George to Port Phillip* (1855) to redress what he considered a slight. Hovell published *A Reply* (1855), and their friendship ended.

In 1860 Hume was elected a fellow of the Royal Geographical Society, and later he served as magistrate until his death.

CHARLES WILKES

(b. April 3, 1798, New York, New York, U.S.—
d. February 8, 1877, Washington, D.C.)

The U.S. naval officer Charles Wilkes explored the region of Antarctica which would be named for him.

Wilkes entered the navy as a midshipman in 1818, became a lieutenant in 1826, and in 1830 was placed in charge of the depot of instruments and charts from which the Naval Observatory and Hydrographic Office developed. From 1838 to 1842 he commanded an exploring and surveying expedition that took him ultimately into the Antarctic Ocean and along the Antarctic barrier, where he reported land at a number of points in the region subsequently known as Wilkes Land. He visited islands in the Pacific, explored the West Coast of the United States, then recrossed the Pacific and reached New York in June 1842, having sailed completely around the world. He was advanced to the rank of commander in 1843. From 1844 to 1861 he prepared the report of his expedition, writing himself 7 of its 19 volumes.

Assigned to the warship *San Jacinto* during the U.S. Civil War (1861–65), Wilkes caused an international incident by stopping the British mail steamer *Trent* (November 8, 1861) and removing two Confederate commissioners en route to Europe. His action was later disavowed by President Lincoln to avoid a break with Great Britain. Commissioned commodore in 1862, he commanded a squadron sent to the West Indies to protect U.S. commerce there. His actions brought protests of neutrality violations from several foreign governments, and he was court-martialed in 1864 for insubordination and conduct unbecoming an officer and suspended from duty. He was commissioned rear admiral, retired, on July 25, 1866.

Wilkes also wrote *Western America, Including California and Oregon* (1849); *Voyage Around the World* (1849); and *Theory of the Winds* (1856).

NATHANIEL PALMER

(b. August 8, 1799, Stonington, Connecticut, U.S.—d. June 21, 1877, San Francisco, California)

Nathaniel Brown Palmer was an American sea captain and explorer after whom Palmer Land, a stretch of western Antarctic coast and islands, is named.

Palmer went to sea at the age of 14. He served first as a sailor on a blockade runner in the War of 1812. He later became a sealer, and his South Sea explorations were largely stimulated by the desire to locate new seal rookeries. Becoming captain of the schooner *Galina* in 1818, Palmer began explorations of the Cape Horn region and western Antarctic the following year. In 1820 he reported a landfall on the coast of Antarctica, which he called Palmer Land. Whether he was the first person to view Antarctica is controversial because Russian explorer Fabian Gottlieb von Bellingshausen and English explorer Edward Bransfield also claimed to have been the first to sight it in 1820. On these and subsequent voyages Palmer discovered the Gerlache Strait and Orleans Channel in Antarctica as well as the South Orkney Islands.

From 1822 to 1826 he engaged in trade on the Spanish Main and helped to transport troops and supplies to Simón Bolívar during the war of South American independence. Throughout much of his career Palmer displayed a keen interest in shipbuilding and helped to design packets (passenger boats), pleasure yachts, and clipper ships.

RENÉ-AUGUSTE CAILLIÉ

(b. November 19, 1799, Mauzé, near La Rochelle, France—d. c. 1838, La Badère)

René-Auguste Caillié was the first European to return from a journey to the West African city of Timbuktu

(Tombouctou). The Scottish explorer Alexander Gordon Laing had reached Timbuktu two years before Caillié, but he had been killed not far from the city on his journey home.

Before Caillié was 20 he had twice voyaged to Senegal and traveled through its interior. In 1824 he began to prepare for his journey to Timbuktu by learning Arabic and studying Islam. Posing as an Arab traveling to Egypt, he left the coast of West Africa in April 1827 and reached Timbuktu on April 20, 1828; his journey was interrupted along the way by five months of illness. He remained at his destination for about two weeks and then returned across the Sahara to France, via Morocco. His narrative of the trip, published in three volumes in 1830, was translated into English that same year. An account of his journey, *The Unveiling of Timbuctoo: The Astounding Adventures of Caillié*, by Galbraith Welch, appeared in 1938.

SIR JAMES CLARK ROSS

(b. April 15, 1800, London, England—d. April 3, 1862, Aylesbury, Buckinghamshire)

The British naval officer Sir James Clark Ross carried out important magnetic surveys in the Arctic and Antarctic and discovered the Ross Sea and the Victoria Land region of Antarctica.

Between 1819 and 1827 Ross accompanied Sir William E. Parry's Arctic voyages. On the second Arctic

James Clark Ross. Hulton Archive/
Getty Images

expedition of his uncle, Sir John Ross, he located the north magnetic pole on June 1, 1831. His own Antarctic expedition of 1839–43 was undertaken to conduct magnetic observations and to reach the south magnetic pole. Commanding the *Erebus* and *Terror*, he discovered the Ross Sea in 1841 and, while sailing toward the position assigned to the magnetic pole, also discovered Victoria Land. He wintered at Hobart, Tasmania, and in November 1841 sailed again for Antarctica. He charted part of the coast of Graham Land and sailed around the Weddell Sea ice. Knighted following his return to England (1843), he published *A Voyage of Discovery and Research in the Southern and Antarctic Regions* (1847).

RICHARD LEMON LANDER

(b. February 8, 1804, Truro, Cornwall,
England—d. February 6, 1834, Fernando Po
[now Bioko, Equatorial Guinea])

Richard Lemon Lander was a British explorer of West Africa who was the first European to trace the course of the lower Niger River to its delta.

He accompanied the Scottish explorer Hugh Clapperton as a servant on his second expedition to the region now lying within northern Nigeria. After Clapperton's death near Sokoto (April 1827), Lander proceeded southeast to Kano and then returned to the coast through the country of the Yoruba people. He published *Journal of Richard Lander from Kano to the Sea Coast* (1829) and *Records of Captain Clapperton's Last Expedition to Africa*, with the Subsequent Adventures of the Author (1830), based on his leader's journal, which he had saved.

At the request of the British government, Lander went again to West Africa. Accompanied by his brother John, he landed at Badagri, now in Nigeria, on March 22, 1830, and traveled inland to Bussa. From there they explored the Niger upstream for about 100 miles (160 km) and then began a hazardous canoe trip downstream to the river's delta. Seized by inhabitants of the delta, the brothers were held captive until a large ransom was paid and passage was secured for them to the island of Fernando Po (now Bioko) in the Bight of Biafra. Their exploration was recounted in

63

Journal of an Expedition to Explore the Course and Termination of the Niger (1832). On a trading expedition up the Niger, Lander was wounded by tribesmen attacking his canoe, and he died soon thereafter.

Drawing of a view of the Maya temple by Frederick Catherwood from John Lloyd Stephens' Incidents of Travel in Central America, Chiapas, and Yucatan, 2 vol. *(1841).* DEA/G. Dagli Orti/De Agostini/Getty Images

JOHN LLOYD STEPHENS

(b. November 28, 1805, Shrewsbury, New
Jersey, U.S.—d. October 12, 1852, New York,
New York)

John Lloyd Stephens was an American traveler and
archaeologist whose exploration of Maya ruins in
Central America and Mexico (1839–40 and 1841–42) gen-
erated the archaeology of Middle America.

Bored with the practice of law and advised to travel
for reasons of health, in 1834 Stephens set out on a journey that took him through eastern Europe and the Middle
East, where he was particularly drawn to many of the
archaeological sites. Two popular books resulted, *Incidents
of Travel in Egypt, Arabia Petraea, and the Holy Land*, 2 vol.
(1837), and *Incidents of Travel in Greece, Turkey, Russia, and
Poland*, 2 vol. (1838), with drawings by the English illustra-
tor and archaeologist Frederick Catherwood.

Reports of the existence of ancient ruins in Central
America and on the Yucatán Peninsula stirred Stephens's
curiosity to locate and explore them. He obtained an
appointment as U.S. chargé d'affaires to Central America
through the influence of President Martin Van Buren, and
in 1839, accompanied by Catherwood, he went to Central
America, then torn by political upheaval and civil war.
Their progress to Copán, Honduras, was imperiled first by
local strife and then by the hazards and extreme hardships
of travel through dense, dark jungle. At times they nearly
despaired of finding what they sought, but their perse-
verance was vastly rewarded. After coming upon a wall of

uncertain significance, they were stunned by the appearance of a magnificently carved stone stela (slab).

Other discoveries—more stelae, terraces, stairways, and walls with strange and fantastic ornamentation—came in quick succession. Stephens "purchased" the extensive site for a modest sum, and work progressed in clearing away the jungle overgrowth. There and elsewhere, including Uxmal and Palenque in Mexico, Catherwood set about drawing the Maya remains. The report of the first expedition, *Incidents of Travel in Central America, Chiapas, and Yucatan*, 2 vol. (1841), and the subsequent publication of Catherwood's superb drawings caused a storm of popular and scholarly interest and precipitated much study of earlier, mostly forgotten accounts of the lands of the Maya by Spanish conquerors and explorers.

After their second expedition, Stephens and Catherwood published *Incidents of Travel in Yucatan*, 2 vol. (1843), containing accounts of visits to the remains of 44 ancient sites. Stephens's last years were devoted to directing the first American transatlantic steamship company and to developing a railroad across the Isthmus of Panama.

SIR ROBERT JOHN LE MESURIER MCCLURE

(b. January 28, 1807, Wexford, County Wexford, Ireland—d. October 17, 1873, London, England)

Sir Robert John Le Mesurier McClure was the Irish naval officer who discovered the long-sought Northwest Passage, the waterway linking the Pacific and Atlantic oceans through Arctic North America. He completed the route, partly by ship and partly overland, during 1850–54.

In 1850 McClure took command of the *Investigator*, one of two ships sent that year to find the British explorer Sir John Franklin, who had been missing in the North American Arctic since 1845. From the Pacific, McClure entered the Bering Strait and, heading eastward north of Alaska, found two entrances to the Northwest Passage around Banks Island, now part of the Northwest Territories of Canada. The *Investigator* became trapped in the ice of Mercy Bay just north of Banks Island, compelling him to abandon the ship, but his party was rescued by two ships at nearby Melville Island. The rescue ships were in turn abandoned, and the party proceeded on foot to Beechey Island and then returned home by ship. McClure was knighted in 1854.

CHARLES DARWIN

(b. February 12, 1809, Shrewsbury, Shropshire, England—d. April 19, 1882, Downe, Kent)

The English naturalist Charles Robert Darwin developed the theory of evolution by natural selection that became the foundation of modern evolutionary studies. An affable country gentleman, Darwin at first shocked religious Victorian society by suggesting that animals and humans shared a common ancestry. His nonreligious biology appealed to the rising class of professional scientists, however, and by the time of his death evolutionary imagery had spread through all of science, literature, and politics. Darwin, himself an agnostic, was accorded the ultimate British accolade of burial in Westminster Abbey in London.

Darwin formulated his bold theory in private in 1837–39, after returning from a voyage around the world aboard HMS *Beagle*, but it was not until two decades later that he finally gave it full public expression in *On the Origin of Species* (1859), a book that has deeply influenced modern Western society and thought.

EARLY LIFE AND EDUCATION

Darwin was the second son of society doctor Robert Waring Darwin and of Susannah Wedgwood, daughter of the Unitarian pottery industrialist Josiah Wedgwood. Darwin's other grandfather, Erasmus Darwin, a free-thinking physician and poet fashionable before the French Revolution, was author of *Zoonomia or the Laws of Organic Life* (1794–96). Darwin's mother died when he was eight, and he was cared for by his three elder sisters. The boy stood in awe of his overbearing father, whose astute medical observations taught him much about human psychology. But he hated the rote learning of Classics at the traditional Anglican Shrewsbury School, where he studied between 1818 and 1825. Science was then considered dehumanizing in English public schools, and for dabbling in chemistry Darwin was condemned by his headmaster (and nicknamed "Gas" by his schoolmates).

His father, considering the 16-year-old a wastrel interested only in game shooting, sent him to study medicine at Edinburgh University in 1825. Later in life, Darwin gave the impression that he had learned little during his two years at Edinburgh. In fact, it was a formative experience.

Charles Darwin, carbon-print photograph by Julia Margaret Cameron, 1868. Royal Photographic Society/ SSPL/Getty Images

There was no better science education in a British university. He was taught to understand the chemistry of cooling rocks on the primitive Earth and how to classify plants by the modern "natural system." In Edinburgh Museum he was taught to stuff birds by a freed South American slave and to identify the rock strata and colonial flora and fauna.

More crucially, the university's radical students exposed the teenager to the latest Continental sciences. Edinburgh attracted English Dissenters who were barred from graduating at the Anglican universities of Oxford and Cambridge, and at student societies Darwin heard freethinkers deny the Divine design of human facial anatomy and argue that animals shared all the human mental faculties. One talk, on the mind as the product of a material brain, was officially censored, for such materialism was considered subversive in the conservative decades after the French Revolution. Darwin was witnessing the social penalties of holding deviant views. As he collected sea slugs and sea pens on nearby shores, he was accompanied by Robert Edmond Grant, a radical evolutionist and disciple of the French biologist Jean-Baptiste Lamarck. An expert on sponges, Grant became Darwin's mentor, teaching him about the growth and relationships of primitive marine invertebrates, which Grant believed held the key to unlocking the mysteries surrounding the origin of more complex creatures. Darwin, encouraged to tackle the larger questions of life through a study of invertebrate zoology, made his own observations on the larval sea mat (*Flustra*) and announced his findings at the student societies.

The young Darwin learned much in Edinburgh's rich intellectual environment, but not medicine: he loathed anatomy, and (pre-chloroform) surgery sickened him. His freethinking father, shrewdly realizing that the church was a better calling for an aimless naturalist, switched him to Christ's College, Cambridge, in 1828. In a complete change of environment, Darwin was now educated as an Anglican gentleman. He took his horse, indulged his drinking, shooting, and beetle-collecting passions with other squires' sons, and managed 10th place in the Bachelor of Arts degree in 1831. Here he was shown the conservative side of botany by a young professor, the Reverend John Stevens Henslow, while that doyen of Providential design in the animal world, the Reverend Adam Sedgwick, took Darwin to Wales in 1831 on a geologic field trip.

Fired by Alexander von Humboldt's account of the South American jungles in his *Personal Narrative of Travels*, Darwin jumped at Henslow's suggestion of a voyage to Tierra del Fuego, at the southern tip of South America, aboard a rebuilt brig, HMS *Beagle*. Darwin would not sail as a lowly surgeon-naturalist but as a self-financed gentleman companion to the 26-year-old captain, Robert Fitzroy, an aristocrat who feared the loneliness of command. Fitzroy's was to be an imperial-evangelical voyage: he planned to survey coastal Patagonia to facilitate British trade and return three "savages" previously brought to England from Tierra del Fuego and Christianized. Darwin equipped himself with weapons, books (Fitzroy gave him the first volume of *Principles of Geology* by the pioneering geologist Charles Lyell, who helped lay the foundation for evolutionary biology), and advice on preserving carcasses from London Zoo's experts. The *Beagle* sailed from England on December 27, 1831.

THE *BEAGLE* VOYAGE

The circumnavigation of the globe would be the making of the 22-year-old Darwin. Five years of physical hardship and mental rigour, imprisoned within a ship's walls, offset by wide-open opportunities in the Brazilian jungles and the Andes Mountains, were to give Darwin a new seriousness. As a gentleman naturalist, he could leave the ship for extended periods, pursuing his own interests. As a result, he spent only 18 months of the voyage aboard the ship.

The hardship was immediate: a tormenting seasickness. And so was his questioning: on calm days Darwin's fine-mesh net that he towed behind the ship would fill with plankton and leave him wondering why beautiful creatures teemed in the ocean's vastness, where no human could appreciate them. On the Cape Verde Islands (January 1832), the sailor saw bands of oyster shells running through local rocks, suggesting that Lyell was right in his geologic speculations and that the land was rising in places, falling in others. At Bahia (now Salvador), Brazil, the luxuriance of the rainforest left Darwin's mind in "a chaos of delight." But that mind, with its Wedgwood-abolitionist characteristics, was revolted by the local slavery. For Darwin, so often alone, the tropical forests seemed to compensate for human evils: months were spent in Rio de Janeiro amid this shimmering tropical splendour, full of "gaily-coloured" flatworms, and the collector himself became "red-hot with Spiders." But nature had its own evils, and Darwin always remembered with a shudder the parasitic ichneumon wasp, which stored caterpillars to be eaten alive by its grubs. He would later consider this evidence against the beneficent design of nature.

On the River Plate (Río de la Plata) in July 1832, he found Montevideo, Uruguay, in a state of rebellion and joined armed sailors to retake the rebel-held fort. At Bahía Blanca, Argentina, gauchos told him of their extermination of the Pampas "Indians." Beneath the veneer of human civility, genocide seemed the rule on the frontier, a conclusion reinforced by Darwin's meeting with General Juan Manuel de Rosas and his "villainous Banditti-like army," in charge of eradicating the natives. For a sensitive young man, fresh from Christ's College, this was disturbing. His contact with "untamed" humans on Tierra del Fuego in December 1832 unsettled him more.

How great, wrote Darwin, the "difference between savage & civilized man is.—It is greater than between a wild & [a] domesticated animal." God had evidently created humans in a vast cultural range, and yet, judging by the Christianized savages aboard, even the "lowest" races were capable of improvement. Darwin was tantalized, and always he sought explanations.

His fossil discoveries raised more questions. Darwin's periodic trips over two years to the cliffs at Bahía Blanca and farther south at Port St. Julian yielded huge bones of extinct mammals. Darwin manhandled skulls, femurs, and armour plates back to the ship—relics, he assumed, of rhinoceroses, mastodons, cow-sized armadillos, and giant ground sloths. He unearthed a horse-sized mammal with a long face like an anteater's, and he returned from a 340-mile (550-km) ride to Mercedes near the Uruguay River with a skull 28 inches (71 cm) long strapped to his horse. Fossil extraction became a romance for Darwin. It pushed him into thinking of the primeval world and what had caused these giant beasts to die out.

The land was evidently changing, rising; Darwin's observations in the Andes Mountains confirmed it. After the *Beagle* surveyed the Falkland Islands, and after Darwin had packed away at Port Desire (Puerto Deseado), Argentina, the partially gnawed bones of a new species of small rhea, the ship sailed up the west coast of South America to Valparaíso, Chile. Here Darwin climbed 4,000 feet (1,200 metres) into the Andean foothills and marveled at the forces that could raise such mountains. The forces themselves became tangible when he saw volcanic Mount Osorno erupt on January 15, 1835. Then in

Valdivia, Chile, on February 20, as he lay on a forest floor, the ground shook: the violence of the earthquake and ensuing tidal wave was enough to destroy the great city of Concepción, whose rubble Darwin walked through. But what intrigued him was the seemingly insignificant: the local mussel beds, all dead, were now lying above high tide. The land had risen: Lyell, taking the uniformitarian position, had argued that geologic formations were the result of steady cumulative forces of the sort we see today. And Darwin had seen them. The continent was thrusting itself up, a few feet at a time. He imagined the eons it had taken to raise the fossilized trees in sandstone (once seashore mud) to 7,000 feet (2,100 metres), where he found them. Darwin began thinking in terms of deep time.

They left Peru on the circumnavigation home in September 1835. First Darwin landed on the "frying hot" Galapagos Islands. These were volcanic prison islands, crawling with marine iguanas and giant tortoises. (Darwin and the crew brought small tortoises aboard as pets, to join their coatis from Peru.) Contrary to legend, these islands never provided Darwin's "eureka" moment. Although he noted that the mockingbirds differed on four islands and tagged his specimens accordingly, he failed to label his other birds—what he thought were wrens, "gross-beaks," finches, and oriole-relatives—by island. Nor did Darwin collect tortoise specimens, even though local prisoners believed that each island had its distinct race.

The "home-sick heroes" returned via Tahiti, New Zealand, and Australia. By April 1836, when the *Beagle* made the Cocos (Keeling) Islands in the Indian Ocean— Fitzroy's brief being to see if coral reefs sat on mountain tops—Darwin already had his theory of reef formation. He imagined (correctly) that these reefs grew on sinking mountain rims. The delicate coral built up, compensating for the drowning land, so as to remain within optimal heat and lighting conditions. At the Cape of Good Hope, Darwin talked with the astronomer Sir John Herschel, possibly about Lyell's gradual geologic evolution and perhaps about how it entailed a new problem, the "mystery of mysteries," the simultaneous change of fossil life.

On the last leg of the voyage Darwin finished his 770-page diary, wrapped up 1,750 pages of notes, drew up 12 catalogs of his 5,436 skins, bones, and carcasses—and still he wondered: Was each Galapagos mockingbird a naturally produced variety? Why did ground sloths become extinct? He sailed home with problems enough to last him a lifetime. When he landed in October 1836, the vicarage had faded, the gun had given way to the notebook, and the supreme theorizer—who would always move from small causes to big outcomes—had the courage to look beyond the conventions of his own Victorian culture for new answers.

EVOLUTION BY NATURAL SELECTION: THE LONDON YEARS, 1836–42

With his voyage over and with a comfortable annual allowance from his father, Darwin now settled down among the urban gentry as a gentleman geologist. He befriended Lyell, and he discussed the rising Chilean coastline as a new fellow of the Geological Society in January 1837 (he was secretary of the society by 1838). Darwin became well known through his diary's publication as *Journal of Researches into the Geology and Natural History of the Various Countries Visited by H.M.S.* Beagle (1839). Using a Treasury grant, obtained through the Cambridge network, he employed the best experts and published their descriptions of his specimens in his *Zoology of the Voyage of H.M.S. Beagle* (1838–43). Darwin's star had risen, and he was now lionized in London.

It was in these years of civil unrest following the Reform Bill of 1832 (which transferred voting privileges from rural areas to the burgeoning industrial cities) that Darwin devised his theory of evolution. Radical Dissenters were denouncing the church's monopoly on power—attacking an Anglican status quo that rested on miraculous props: the supposed supernatural creation of life and society. Darwin had Unitarian roots, and his breathless notes show how his radical Dissenting under-standing of equality and antislavery framed his image of mankind's place in nature: "Animals—whom we have made our slaves we do not like to consider our equals.— Do not slave holders wish to make the black man other kind?" Some radicals questioned whether each animal was uniquely "designed" by God when all vertebrates shared a similar structural plan. The polymathic Charles Babbage—of calculating machine fame—made God a divine programmer, preordaining life by means of natural law rather than ad hoc miracle. It was the ultra-Whig way, and in 1837 Darwin, an impeccable Whig reformer who enjoyed Babbage's soirees, likewise accepted that "the Creator creates by...laws."

The experts' findings sent Darwin to more heretical depths. At the Royal College of Surgeons, the eminent anatomist Richard Owen found that Darwin's Uruguay River skull belonged to Toxodon, a hippopotamus-sized antecedent of the South American capybara. The Pampas fossils were nothing like rhinoceroses and mastodons; they were huge extinct armadillos, anteaters, and sloths, which suggested that South American mammals had been replaced by their own kind according to some unknown "law of succession." At the Zoological Society, ornithologist

John Gould announced that the Galapagos birds were not a mixture of wrens, finches, and "gross-beaks" but were all ground finches, differently adapted. When Gould diagnosed the Galapagos mockingbirds as three species, unique to different islands, in March 1837, Darwin examined Fitzroy's collection to discover that each island had its representative finch as well. But how had they all diverged from mainland colonists? By this time Darwin was living near his freethinking brother, Erasmus, in London's West End, and their dissident dining circle, which included the Unitarian Harriet Martineau, provided the perfect milieu for Darwin's ruminations. Darwin adopted "transmutation" (evolution, as it is now called), perhaps because of his familiarity with it through the work of his grandfather and Robert Grant. Nonetheless, it was abominated by the Cambridge clerics as a bestial, if not blasphemous, heresy that would corrupt mankind and destroy the spiritual safeguards of the social order. Thus began Darwin's double life, which would last for two decades.

For two years he filled notebooks with jottings. There was an intensity and doggedness to it. He searched for the causes of extinction, accepted life as a branching tree, tackled island isolation, and wondered whether variations appeared gradually or at a stroke. Darwin disagreed with the Lamarckian theory that passing on acquired traits was the force driving life inexorably upward, dismissing it with the cavalier joke, "If all men were dead then monkeys make men. — Men make angels." His quip showed how little the failed ordinand shared his Cambridge mentors' hysteria about an ape ancestry. Indeed, there was no "upward": he became relativistic, sensing that life was spreading outward into niches, not standing on a ladder. There was no way of ranking humans and bees, no yardstick of "highness": man was no longer the crown of creation.

Heart palpitations and stomach problems were affecting him by September 1837. Stress sent him to the Highlands of Scotland in 1838, where he diverted himself studying the "parallel roads" of Glen Roy, so like the raised beaches in Chile. But the sickness returned as he continued chipping at the scientific bedrock of a cleric-dominated society. The "whole [miraculous] fabric totters & falls," he jotted. Darwin had a right to be worried. Were his secret discovered, he would stand accused of social abandon. At Edinburgh he had seen censorship; other materialists were being publicly disgraced. His notes began mooting disarming ploys: "Mention persecution of early astronomers." Behind his respectable facade at the Geological Society lay a new contempt for the divines' providential shortsightedness. The president, the Reverend William Whewell, "says length of days adapted to duration of sleep of man.!!!" he jotted. What "arrogance!!"

Mankind: there was the crux. Darwin wrote humans and society into the evolutionary equation from the start. He saw the social instincts of troop animals developing into morality and studied the humanlike behaviour of orangutans at the zoo. With avant-garde society radicalized, Darwin moved into his own ultraradical phase in 1838—even suggesting that belief in God was an ingrained tribal survival strategy: "love of [the] deity [is an] effect of [the brain's] organization. Oh you Materialist!" he mocked himself. In a day when a gentleman's character had to be above reproach, Darwin's notes had a furtive ring. None of this could become known—yet. The rich careerist—admitted to the prestigious Athenaeum Club in 1838 and the Royal Society in 1839—had too much to lose.

As a sporting gent from the shires, Darwin queried breeders about the way they changed domestic dogs and fancy pigeons by spotting slight variations and accentuating them through breeding. But he only saw the complete congruity between the way nature operated and the way

fanciers produced new breeds upon reading the economist Thomas Malthus's *Essay on the Principle of Population*
in September 1838. This was a seminal moment—even
if Malthusian ideas had long permeated his Whig circle.
Darwin was living through a workhouse revolution.
Malthus had said that there would always be too many
mouths to feed—population increases geometrically,
whereas food production rises arithmetically—and that
charity was useless. So the Whigs had passed a Malthusian
Poor Law in 1834 and were incarcerating sick paupers in
workhouses (separating men from women to stop them
from breeding). Darwin's dining companion Harriet
Martineau (whom many expected to marry his brother,
Erasmus), was the Whigs' poor law propagandist. (Her
novelistic Malthusian pamphlets had been sent to Darwin
while he was on the *Beagle*.) Darwin realized that population explosions would lead to a struggle for resources and
that the ensuing competition would weed out the unfit.
It was an idea he now applied to nature (he had previously thought that animal populations remained stable in
the wild). Darwin called his modified Malthusian mechanism "natural selection." Nature was equally uncharitable,
went the argument: overpopulated, it experienced a fierce
struggle, and from all manner of chance variations, good
and bad, the best, "the surviving one of ten thousand tri-
als," won out, endured, and thus passed on its improved
trait. This was the way a species kept pace with the Lyellian
evolution of the Earth.

Darwin was a born list maker. In 1838 he even totted
up the pros and cons of taking a wife—and married his
cousin Emma Wedgwood (1808–96) in 1839. He rashly
confided his thoughts on evolution, evidently shocking
her. By now, Darwin accepted the notion that even mental
traits and instincts were randomly varying, that they were
the stuff for selection. But he saw from Emma's reaction

that he must publicly camouflage his views. Although the randomness and destructiveness of his evolutionary system—with thousands dying so that the "fittest" might survive—left little room for a personally operating benign deity, Darwin still believed that God was the ultimate lawgiver of the universe. In 1839 he shut his last major evolution notebook, his theory largely complete.

THE SQUIRE NATURALIST IN DOWNE

Darwin drafted a 35-page sketch of his theory of natural selection in 1842 and expanded it in 1844, but he had no immediate intention of publishing it. He wrote Emma a letter in 1844 requesting that, if he died, she should pay an editor £400 to publish the work. Perhaps he wanted to die first. In 1842, Darwin, increasingly shunning society, had moved the family to the isolated village of Downe, in Kent, at the "extreme edge of [the] world." (It was in fact only 16 miles [26 km] from central London.) Here, living in a former parsonage, Down House, he emulated the lifestyle of his clerical friends. Fearing prying eyes, he even lowered the road outside his house. His seclusion was complete: from now on he ran his days like clockwork, with set periods for walking, napping, reading, and nightly backgammon. He fulfilled his parish responsibilities, eventually helping to run the local Coal and Clothing Club for the labourers. His work hours were given over to bees, flowers, and barnacles and to his books on coral reefs and South American geology, three of which in 1842–46 secured his reputation as a career geologist.

He rarely mentioned his secret. When he did, notably to the Kew Gardens botanist Joseph Dalton Hooker, Darwin said that believing in evolution was "like confessing a murder." The analogy with this capital offense was not so strange: seditious atheists were using evolution as part of their weaponry against Anglican oppression and were being jailed for blasphemy. Darwin, nervous and nauseous, trying spas and quack remedies (even tying plate batteries to his heaving stomach), understood the conservative clerical morality. He was sensitive to the offense he might cause. He was also immensely wealthy: by the late 1840s the Darwins had a vast fortune invested; he was an absentee landlord of two large Lincolnshire farms; and in the 1850s he plowed another great sum into railway shares. Even though his theory, with its capitalist and meritocratic emphasis, was quite unlike anything touted by the radicals and rioters, these turbulent years were no time to break cover.

From 1846 to 1854, Darwin added to his credibility as an expert on species by pursuing a detailed study of all known barnacles. Intrigued by their sexual differentiation, he discovered that some females had tiny degenerate males clinging to them. This sparked his interest in the evolution of diverging male and female forms from an original hermaphrodite creature. Four monographs on such an obscure group made him a world expert and gained him the Royal Society's Royal Medal in 1853. No longer could he be dismissed as a speculator on biological matters.

ON THE ORIGIN OF SPECIES

England became quieter and more prosperous in the 1850s, and by mid-decade the professionals were taking over, instituting exams and establishing a meritocracy. The changing social composition of science—typified by the rise of the freethinking biologist Thomas Henry Huxley—promised a better reception for Darwin. Huxley,

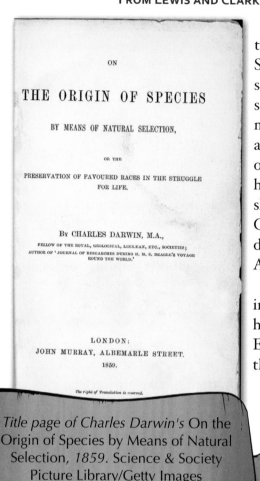

ON

THE ORIGIN OF SPECIES

BY MEANS OF NATURAL SELECTION,

OR THE

PRESERVATION OF FAVOURED RACES IN THE STRUGGLE
FOR LIFE.

By CHARLES DARWIN, M.A.,

FELLOW OF THE ROYAL, GEOLOGICAL, LINNÆAN, ETC., SOCIETIES;
AUTHOR OF 'JOURNAL OF RESEARCHES DURING H. M. S. BEAGLE'S VOYAGE
ROUND THE WORLD.'

LONDON:
JOHN MURRAY, ALBEMARLE STREET.
1859.

The right of Translation is reserved.

Title page of Charles Darwin's On the Origin of Species by Means of Natural Selection, *1859.* Science & Society Picture Library/Getty Images

the philosopher Herbert Spencer, and other outsiders were opting for a secular nature in the rationalist *Westminster Review* and deriding the influence of "parsondom." Darwin had himself lost the last shreds of his belief in Christianity with the tragic death of his oldest daughter, Annie, from typhoid in 1851.

The world was becoming safer for Darwin and his theory: mid-Victorian England was stabler than the "hungry Thirties" or turbulent 1840s. In 1854 he solved his last major problem, the forking of genera to produce new evolutionary branches. He used an industrial analogy familiar from the famous Wedgwood ceramics factories, the division of labour: competition in nature's overcrowded marketplace would favour variants that could exploit different aspects of a niche. Species would diverge on the spot, like tradesmen in the same tenement. Through 1855 Darwin experimented with seeds in seawater, to prove that they could survive ocean crossings to start the process of speciation on islands. Then he kept fancy pigeons, to see if the chicks were more like the ancestral rock dove than their own bizarre parents. Darwin perfected his analogy of natural selection with the fancier's "artificial selection," as he called it. He was preparing his rhetorical strategy, ready to present his theory.

After speaking to Huxley and Hooker at Downe in April 1856, Darwin began writing a triple-volume book, tentatively called *Natural Selection*, which was designed to crush the opposition with a welter of facts. Darwin now had immense scientific and social authority, and his place in the parish was assured when he was sworn in as a justice of the peace in 1857. Encouraged by Lyell, Darwin continued writing through the birth of his 10th and last child, the mentally retarded Charles Waring Darwin (born in 1856, when Emma was 48). Whereas in the 1830s Darwin had thought that species remained perfectly adapted until the environment changed, he now believed that every new variation was imperfect, and that perpetual struggle was the rule. He also explained the evolution of sterile worker bees in 1857. These could not be selected because they did not breed, so he opted for "family" selection (kin selection, as it is known today): the whole colony benefited from their retention.

Darwin had finished a quarter of a million words by June 18, 1858. That day he received a letter from Alfred Russel Wallace, an English socialist and specimen collector working in the Malay Archipelago, sketching a similar-looking theory. Darwin, fearing loss of priority, accepted Lyell's and Hooker's solution: they read joint extracts from Darwin's and Wallace's works at the Linnean Society on July 1, 1858. Darwin was away, sick, grieving for his tiny son who had died from scarlet fever, and thus he missed the first public presentation of the theory of natural selection. It was an absenteeism that would mark his later years.

Darwin hastily began an "abstract" of *Natural Selection*, which grew into a more accessible book, *On the Origin of Species by Means of Natural Selection, or the Preservation of*

"Gorilla: 'That Man wants to claim my Pedigree. He says he is one of my Descendants.'"

"Mr. Bergh [founder of the A. S. P. C. A.]: 'Now, Mr. Darwin, how could you insult him so?'"

Contemporary cartoon by Thomas Nast.

Satirical cartoon by Thomas Nast, from Harper's Weekly, *August 19, 1871. Victorian society was shocked by the publication in 1859 of Charles Darwin's* Origin of Species *and in 1871 of his* Descent of Man, *both of which seemed to indicate that man was descended from the apes. Here the artist puts all the dismay into the mouth of the "defrauded" ape. Fotosearch/Archive Photos/Getty Images*

Favoured Races in the Struggle for Life. Suffering from a terrible bout of nausea, Darwin, now 50, was secreted away at a spa on the desolate Yorkshire moors when the book was sold to the trade on November 22, 1859. He still feared the worst and sent copies to the experts with self-effacing letters ("how you will long to crucify me alive"). It was like "living in Hell," he said about these months.

The book did distress his Cambridge patrons, but they were marginal to science now. Radical Dissenters were sympathetic, however, as were the rising London biologists and geologists, even if few actually adopted Darwin's cost-benefit approach to nature. The newspapers drew the one conclusion that Darwin had specifically avoided: that humans had evolved from apes, and that Darwin was denying mankind's immortality. A sensitive Darwin, making no personal appearances, let Huxley, by now a good friend, manage this part of the debate. The pugnacious Huxley, who loved public argument as much as Darwin loathed it, had his own reasons for taking up the cause, and did so with enthusiasm. He wrote three reviews of *Origin of Species*, defended human evolution at the Oxford meeting of the British Association for the Advancement of Science in 1860 (when Bishop Samuel Wilberforce jokingly asked whether the apes were on Huxley's grandmother's or grandfather's side), and published his own book on human evolution, *Evidence as to Man's Place in Nature* (1863). What Huxley championed was Darwin's evolutionary naturalism, his nonmiraculous assumptions, which pushed biological science into previously taboo areas and increased the power of Huxley's professionals. And it was they who gained the Royal Society's Copley Medal for Darwin in 1864.

Huxley's reaction, with its enthusiasm for evolution and cooler opinion of natural selection, was typical. Natural selection—the "law of higgledy-piggledy" in Herschel's dismissive words—received little support in Darwin's day. By contrast, evolution itself ("descent," Darwin called it—the word *evolution* would only be introduced in the last, 1872, edition of the *Origin*) was being acknowledged from British Association platforms by 1866. That year, too, Darwin met his German admirer, the zoologist Ernst Haeckel, whose proselytizing would spread Darwinismus through the Prussian world. Two years later the King of Prussia conferred on Darwin the order *Pour le Mérite*.

THE PATRIARCH IN HIS HOME LABORATORY

Long periods of debilitating sickness in the 1860s left the craggy, bearded Darwin thin and ravaged. He once vomited for 27 consecutive days. Down House was an infirmary where illness was the norm and Emma the attendant nurse. She was a shield, protecting the patriarch, cosseting him. Darwin was a typical Victorian in his racial and sexual stereotyping—however dependent on his redoubtable wife, he still thought women inferior; and although a fervent abolitionist, he still considered blacks a lower race. But few outside of the egalitarian socialists challenged these prejudices—and Darwin, immersed in a competitive Whig culture, and enshrining its values in his science, had no time for socialism.

The house was also a laboratory, where Darwin continued experimenting and revamping the *Origin* through six editions. Although quietly swearing by "my deity 'Natural Selection,'" he answered critics by reemphasizing other causes of change—for example, the effects of continued use of an organ—and he bolstered the Lamarckian belief that such alterations through excessive use might be passed on. In *Variation of Animals and Plants under Domestication* (1868) he marshaled the facts and explored the causes of variation in domestic breeds. The book answered critics such as George Douglas Campbell, the eighth duke of Argyll, who loathed Darwin's blind, accidental process of variation and envisaged the appearance of "new births" as goal directed. By showing that fanciers picked from the gamut of naturally occurring variations to produce the tufts and topknots on their fancy pigeons, Darwin undermined this providential explanation.

In 1867 the engineer Fleeming Jenkin argued that any single favourable variation would be swamped and lost by back-breeding within the general population. No mechanism was known for inheritance, and so in the *Variation* Darwin devised his hypothesis of "pangenesis" to explain the discrete inheritance of traits. He imagined that each tissue of an organism threw out tiny "gemmules," which passed to the sex organs and permitted copies of themselves to be made in the next generation. But Darwin's cousin Francis Galton failed to find these gemmules in rabbit blood, and the theory was dismissed.

Darwin was adept at flanking movements in order to get around his critics. He would take seemingly intractable subjects—such as orchid flowers—and make them test cases for "natural selection." Hence the book that appeared after the *Origin* was, to everyone's surprise, *The Various Contrivances by which British and Foreign Orchids are Fertilised by Insects* (1862). He showed that the orchid's beauty was not a piece of floral whimsy "designed" by God to please humans but honed by selection to attract insect cross-pollinators. The petals guided the bees to the nectaries, and pollen sacs were deposited exactly where they could be removed by a stigma of another flower.

But why the importance of cross-pollination? Darwin's botanical work was always subtly related to his evolutionary mechanism. He believed that cross-pollinated plants would produce fitter offspring than self-pollinators, and he used considerable ingenuity in conducting thousands of crossings to prove the point. The results appeared in *The Effects of Cross and Self Fertilization in the Vegetable Kingdom* (1876). His next book, *The Different Forms of Flowers on Plants of the Same Species* (1877), was again the result of long-standing work into the way evolution in some species favoured different male and female forms of flowers to facilitate outbreeding. Darwin had long been sensitive to the effects of inbreeding because he was himself married to a Wedgwood cousin, as was his sister Caroline. He agonized over its debilitating consequence for his five sons who had survived to adulthood. Not that he need have worried, for they fared well: William became a banker, Leonard an army major, George the Plumian Professor of Astronomy at Cambridge, Francis a reader in botany at Cambridge, and Horace a scientific instrument maker. Darwin also studied insectivorous plants, climbing plants, and the response of plants to gravity and light (sunlight, he thought, activated something in the shoot tip, an idea that guided future work on growth hormones in plants).

THE PRIVATE MAN AND THE PUBLIC DEBATE

Through the 1860s natural selection was already being applied to the growth of society. A.R. Wallace saw cooperation strengthening the moral bonds within primitive tribes. Advocates of social Darwinism, in contrast, complained that modern civilization was protecting the "unfit" from natural selection. Francis Galton argued that particular character traits—even drunkenness and genius—were inherited and that "eugenics," as it would come to be called, would stop the genetic drain. The trend to explain the evolution of human races, morality, and civilization was capped by Darwin in his two-volume *The Descent of Man, and Selection in Relation to Sex* (1871). The book was authoritative, annotated, and heavily anecdotal in places. The two volumes were discrete, the first discussing the evolution of civilization and human origins among the Old World monkeys. (Darwin's depiction of a hairy human ancestor with pointed ears led to a spate of caricatures in newspapers and periodicals.) The second volume responded to critics such as Argyll, who doubted that the iridescent hummingbird's plumage had any function—or any Darwinian explanation. Darwin argued that female birds were choosing mates for their gaudy plumage. Darwin as usual tapped his huge correspondence network of breeders, naturalists, and travelers worldwide to produce evidence for this. Such "sexual selection" happened among humans too. With primitive societies accepting diverse notions of beauty, aesthetic preferences, he believed, could account for the origin of the human races.

Darwin's explanation was also aimed partly at Wallace. Like so many disillusioned socialists, Wallace had become engaged in spiritualism. He argued that an overdeveloped human brain had been provided by the spirit forces to move humanity toward millennial perfection. Darwin had no time for this. Even though he eventually attended a séance with Galton and the novelist George Eliot (Marian Evans) at his brother's house in 1874, he was appalled at "such rubbish," and in 1876 he sent £10 toward the costs of the prosecution of the medium Henry Slade.

Darwin finished another long-standing line of work. Since studying the moody orangutans at London Zoo in 1838, through the births of his 10 children (whose facial contortions he duly noted), Darwin had been fascinated by expression. As a student he had heard the attacks on the idea that peoples' facial muscles were designed by God to express their unique thoughts. Now his photographically illustrated *The Expression of the Emotions in Man and Animals* (1872) expanded the subject to include the rages and grimaces of asylum inmates, all to show the continuity of emotions and expressions between humans and animals.

The gentle Darwin elicited tremendous devotion. A protective circle formed around him, locked tight by Huxley and Hooker. It was they who ostracized detractors, particularly the Roman Catholic zoologist Saint George Jackson Mivart. Nor did Darwin forget it: he helped raise funds to send a fatigued Huxley on holiday in 1873, and his pestering resulted in the impecunious Wallace being added to the Civil List (i.e., granted a royal pension) in 1881. Darwin was held in awe by many, the more so because he was rarely seen. And when he was seen—for example, by the Harvard philosopher John Fiske, a privileged visitor to Down House in 1873—he was found to be "the dearest, sweetest, loveliest old grandpa that ever was."

Darwin wrote his autobiography between 1876 and 1881. It was composed for his grandchildren, rather than for publication, and it was particularly candid on his dislike of Christian myths of eternal torment. To people who inquired about his religious beliefs, however, he would only say that he was an agnostic (a word coined by Huxley in 1869).

The treadmill of experiment and writing gave so much meaning to his life. But as he wrapped up his final, long-term interest, publishing *The Formation of Vegetable Mould, Through the Action of Worms* (1881), the future looked bleak. Such an earthy subject was typical Darwin: just as he had shown that today's ecosystems were built by infinitesimal degrees and the mighty Andes by tiny uplifts, so he ended on the monumental transformation of landscapes by the Earth's humblest denizens.

Suffering from angina, he looked forward to joining the worms, contemplating "Down graveyard as the sweetest place on earth." He had a seizure in March 1882 and died of a heart attack on April 19. Influential groups wanted a grander commemoration than a funeral in Downe, something better for the gentleman naturalist who had delivered the "new Nature" into the new professionals' hands. Galton had the Royal Society request the family's permission for a state burial. Huxley, who by taking over the public debate had preserved Darwin's reputation of "sweet and gentle nature blossomed into perfection," as a newspaper put it, convinced the canon of Westminster Abbey to bury the diffident agnostic there. And so Darwin was laid to rest with full ecclesiastical pomp on April 26, 1882, attended by the new nobility of science and the state.

NIKOLAY NIKOLAYEVICH AMURSKY, GRAF MURAVYOV

(b. August 11 [August 23, New Style], 1809,
St. Petersburg, Russia—d. November 18
[November 30], 1881, Paris, France)

Nikolay Nikolayevich Amursky, Graf Muravyov (or Muraviev) was the Russian statesman and explorer whose efforts led to the expansion of the Russian Empire to the Pacific Ocean. In 1860 he planted the Russian flag at what was to become the port of Vladivostok.

A lieutenant general in the Russian army, Muravyov was appointed governor-general of eastern Siberia in 1847. Despite the opposition of many in the tsarist government who feared the reaction of the Chinese, he vigorously pursued the exploration and settlement of Siberia north of the Amur River. In the period 1854–58 he led a number of expeditions down the Amur, during the last of which, having obtained plenipotentiary powers from the tsar, he concluded the Treaty of Aigun with China (1858). This pact recognized the Amur as the boundary between Russia and China and greatly expanded Russian territory in Siberia. For his role Muravyov was granted the title of Count Amursky. The peninsula on which Vladivostok lies still bears his name.

Muravyov proposed the construction of a trans-Siberian railway several decades before its accomplishment. He also suggested that Alaska be ceded to the United States.

JOHN C. FRÉMONT

(b. January 21, 1813, Savannah, Georgia,
U.S.—d. July 13, 1890, New York, New York)

The American mapmaker and explorer of the Far West John Charles Frémont was an important figure in the U.S. conquest and development of California. He ran unsuccessfully as the first Republican presidential candidate in 1856.

In 1838 Frémont assisted the French scientist Jean-Nicolas Nicollet in surveying and mapping the upper Mississippi and Missouri rivers. He also headed an expedition (1841) to survey the Des Moines River for Nicollet, who had given him expert instruction in geology, topography, and astronomy. His growing taste for wilderness

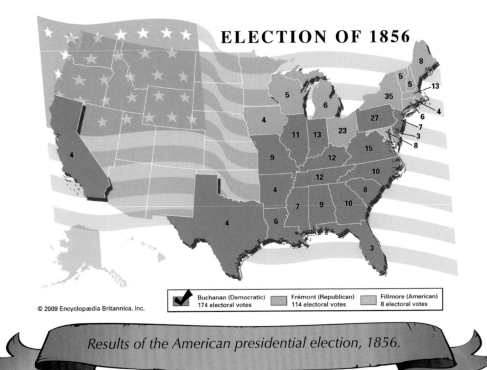

ELECTION OF 1856

Buchanan (Democratic)
174 electoral votes

Frémont (Republican)
114 electoral votes

Fillmore (American)
8 electoral votes

Results of the American presidential election, 1856.

exploration was whetted by the expansionist enthusiasm of Missouri senator Thomas Hart Benton, who became his adviser, sponsor, and, in 1841, father-in-law. Benton's influence in government enabled Frémont to accomplish within the next few years the mapping of much of the territory between the Mississippi valley and the Pacific Ocean. In 1842 the War Department sent him to survey the route west to Wyoming, and in 1843, accompanied by the colourful guide Kit Carson and mountain man Thomas Fitzpatrick, he completed a survey to the mouth of the Columbia River. After thoroughly exploring much of the Northwest, he made a winter crossing of the Sierra Nevada to California, further adding to his fame.

War with Mexico over the annexation of Texas seemed imminent, and in the spring of 1845 Frémont headed a third expedition west with secret instructions for action in case of war. Upon his arrival in southern California at the end of the year, he and his armed party defied Mexican authorities before standing down and heading north into what is now southern Oregon. He and his group soon returned south in early May 1846, however, after receiving a still-unknown message from a confidential messenger from Washington. Back in California, he threw his support behind a small group of dissident Americans near Sonoma who had started an unofficial uprising and had established the short-lived Bear Flag Republic. News of the declaration of war with Mexico soon reached California, and Frémont was appointed by Commodore Robert F. Stockton as major of a battalion of mostly American volunteers and, with Stockton, completed the conquest of the future 31st state. Meanwhile, General Stephen Watts Kearny entered California from the southeast with orders to establish a government, leading to an obvious conflict of authority. Frémont accepted California's capitulation from Mexican officials at Cahuenga Pass, near Los Angeles, and Stockton appointed him military governor of California. Kearny, however, had Frémont arrested and court-martialed in Washington, D.C., in 1847–48 for disobedience. He was sentenced to dismissal from the army, and although his penalty was set aside by President James K. Polk, Frémont resigned. Through it all, he retained the high regard of the general public.

Frémont became a multimillionaire in the 1848 California gold bonanza, and in 1850 he was elected one of the state's first two senators. A firm opponent of slavery, he was nominated for the presidency in 1856 by the new Republican Party. In the election he was defeated by the Democratic candidate, James Buchanan, but he came closer to uniting the electorate of the North and West against the South than had any previous candidate.

Frémont served unsuccessfully as a Union officer in the American Civil War, and he resigned from the army (1862) for a second time. Still popular, he was considered for the presidential nomination again in 1864 but withdrew to avoid dividing the party. Thereafter he retired from public life to devote himself to railroad projects in the West. In 1878, after losing his fortune, he was appointed governor of the Arizona Territory, where he served until 1883.

DAVID LIVINGSTONE

(b. March 19, 1813, Blantyre, Lanarkshire, Scotland—d. May 1, 1873, Chitambo [now in Zambia])

The Scottish missionary and explorer David Livingstone exercised a formative influence on Western attitudes toward Africa through his many expeditions to the continent. His rescue in eastern Africa by Henry M. Stanley in 1871 became one of the most famous episodes in the history of European exploration.

EARLY LIFE

Livingstone grew up in a distinctively Scottish family environment of personal piety, poverty, hard work, zeal for education, and a sense of mission. His father's family was from the island of Ulva, off the west coast of Scotland. His mother, a Lowlander, was descended from a family of Covenanters, a group of militant Presbyterians. Both were poor, and Livingstone was reared as one of seven children in a single room at the top of a tenement building for the workers of a cotton factory on the banks of the Clyde.

David Livingstone. Photos.com/Thinkstock

At age 10 he had to help his family and was put to work in a cotton mill, and with part of his first week's wages he bought a Latin grammar. Although he was brought up in the Calvinist faith of the established Scottish church, Livingstone, like his father, joined an independent Christian congregation of stricter discipline when he came to manhood. By this time he had acquired those

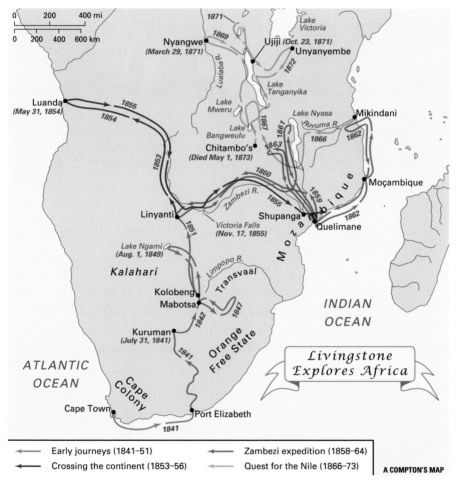

Explorations of David Livingstone.

David Livingstone's expedition to Lake Ngami (now in Botswana), 19th-century chromolithograph. Photos.com/ Thinkstock

characteristics of mind and body that were to fit him for his African career.

In 1834 an appeal by British and American churches for qualified medical missionaries in China made Livingstone determined to pursue that profession. To prepare himself, while continuing to work part-time in the mill, he studied Greek, theology, and medicine for two years in Glasgow. In 1838 he was accepted by the London Missionary Society. The first of the Opium Wars (1839–42) put an end to his dreams of going to China, but a meeting with Robert Moffat, the notable Scottish missionary in southern Africa, convinced him that Africa should be his sphere of service. On November 20, 1840, he was ordained as a missionary; he set sail for South Africa at the end of the year and arrived at Cape Town on March 14, 1841.

INITIAL EXPLORATIONS

For the next 15 years, Livingstone was constantly on the move into the African interior: strengthening his missionary determination; responding wholeheartedly to the delights of geographic discovery; clashing with the Boers (South Africans of Dutch ancestry) and the Portuguese, whose treatment of the Africans he came to detest; and building for himself a remarkable reputation as a dedicated Christian, a courageous explorer, and a fervent antislavery advocate. Yet so impassioned was his commitment to Africa that his duties as husband and father were relegated to second place.

From Moffat's mission at Kuruman on the Cape frontier, which Livingstone reached on July 31, 1841, he soon pushed his search for converts northward into untried country where the population was reputed to be more numerous. This suited his purpose of spreading the Gospel through "native agents." By the summer of 1842, he had already gone farther north than any other European into the difficult Kalahari country and had familiarized himself with the local languages and cultures. His mettle was dramatically tested in 1844 when, during a journey to Mabotsa to establish a mission station, he was mauled by a lion. The resulting injury to his left arm was complicated by another accident, and he could never again support the barrel of a gun steadily with his left hand and thus was obliged to fire from his left shoulder and to take aim with his left eye.

On January 2, 1845, Livingstone married Moffat's daughter, Mary, and she accompanied him on many of his journeys until her health and the family's needs for security and education forced him to send her and their four children back to Britain in 1852. Before this first parting with his family, Livingstone had already achieved a small

Victoria Falls on the Zambezi River as seen from Zambia.
G. Holton/Photo Researchers

measure of fame as surveyor and scientist of a small expedition responsible for the first European sighting of Lake Ngami (August 1, 1849), for which he was awarded a gold medal and monetary prize by the British Royal Geographical Society. This recognition of his achievement was the beginning of his lifelong association with the society, which continued to encourage his ambitions as an explorer and to champion his interests in Britain.

OPENING THE INTERIOR

With his family safely in Scotland, Livingstone was ready to push Christianity, commerce, and civilization—the trinity that he believed was destined to open up Africa—northward beyond the frontiers of South Africa and into the heart of the continent. In a famous statement in 1853 he made his purpose clear: "I shall open up a path into the interior, or perish." On November 11, 1853, from Linyanti at the approaches to the Zambezi River and in the midst of the Makololo peoples whom he considered eminently suitable for missionary work, Livingstone set out northwestward with little equipment and only a small party of Africans. His intention was to find a route to the Atlantic coast that would permit legitimate commerce to undercut the slave trade and that would also be more suitable

for reaching the Makololo than the route leading through
Boer territory. (In 1852 the Boers had destroyed his home at
Kolobeng and attacked his African friends.) After an arduous journey that might have wrecked the constitution of a
lesser man, Livingstone reached Luanda on the west coast on
May 31, 1854. In order to take his Makololo followers back
home and to carry out further explorations of the Zambezi,
as soon as his health permitted—on September 20, 1854—
he began the return journey. He reached Linyanti nearly
a year later on September 11, 1855. Continuing eastward on
November 3, Livingstone explored the Zambezi regions
and reached Quelimane in Mozambique on May 20, 1856.
His most spectacular visit on this last leg of his great journey was to the thundering, smokelike waters on the Zambezi
at which he arrived on November 17, 1855, and with typical
patriotism (and, perhaps, equal parts British ethnocentrism)
named Victoria Falls for his queen. Livingstone returned to
England on December 9, 1856, a national hero. News from
and about him during the previous three years had stirred
the imagination of English-speaking peoples everywhere to
an unprecedented degree.

Livingstone recorded his accomplishments modestly
but effectively in his *Missionary Travels and Researches in
South Africa* (1857), which quickly sold more than 70,000
copies and took its place in publishing history as well as
in that of exploration and missionary endeavour. Honours
flowed in upon him. His increased income meant that he
was now able to provide adequately for his family, which
had lived in near poverty since returning to Britain. He
was also able to make himself independent of the London
Missionary Society. After the completion of his book,
Livingstone spent six months speaking throughout the
British Isles. In his Senate House address at Cambridge
on December 4, 1857, he foresaw that he would be unable
to complete his work in Africa, and he called on young

university men to take up the task that he had begun. The publication of *Dr. Livingstone's Cambridge Lectures* (1858) roused almost as much interest as his book, and out of his Cambridge visit came the Universities' Mission to Central Africa in 1860, on which Livingstone set high hopes during his second expedition to Africa.

THE ZAMBEZI EXPEDITION

This time Livingstone was away from Britain from March 12, 1858, to July 23, 1864. He went out originally as British consul at Quelimane:

> *for the Eastern Coast and independent districts of the interior, and commander of an expedition for exploring eastern and central Africa, for the promotion of Commerce and Civilization with a view to the extinction of the slave-trade.*

This expedition was infinitely better organized than Livingstone's previous solitary journeys. It had a paddle steamer, impressive stores, 10 Africans, and 6 Europeans (including his brother Charles and an Edinburgh doctor, John Kirk). That Livingstone's by then legendary leadership had its limitations was soon revealed. Quarrels broke out among the Europeans, and some were dismissed. Disillusionment with Livingstone set in among members both of his own expedition and of the abortive Universities' Mission that followed it to central Africa. It proved impossible to navigate the Zambezi by ship, and Livingstone's two attempts to find a route along the Ruvuma River bypassing Portuguese territory to districts around Lake Nyasa (Lake Malawi) also proved impractical. Livingstone and his party had been the first Britons to reach (September 17, 1859) these districts that held out promise of colonization. Compounding Livingstone's troubles with the expedition, he was left grief-stricken when his wife, who had been determined to accompany him back to Africa, died at Shupanga on the Zambezi on April 27, 1862. In addition, his eldest son, Robert, who was to have joined his father in 1863, never reached him and went instead to the United States, where he died fighting for the North in the Civil War on December 5, 1864.

The British government recalled the expedition in 1863, when it was clear that Livingstone's optimism about economic and political developments in the Zambezi regions was premature. Livingstone, however, showed something of his old fire when he took his little vessel, the *Lady Nyassa*, with a small untrained crew and little fuel, on a hazardous voyage of 2,500 miles (4,000 km) across the Indian Ocean and left it for sale in Bombay (now Mumbai). Furthermore, within the next three decades the Zambezi expedition proved to be anything but a disaster. It had amassed a valuable body of scientific knowledge, and the association of the Lake Nyasa regions with Livingstone's name and the prospects for colonization that he envisaged there were important factors for the creation in 1893 of the British Central Africa Protectorate, which in 1907 became Nyasaland and in 1966 the republic of Malawi.

Back in Britain in the summer of 1864, Livingstone, with his brother Charles, wrote his second book, *Narrative of an Expedition to the Zambesi and Its Tributaries* (1865). Livingstone was advised at this time to have a surgical operation for the hemorrhoids that had troubled him since his first great African journey. He refused, and it is probable that severe bleeding hemorrhoids were the cause of his death at the end of his third and greatest African journey.

QUEST FOR THE NILE

Livingstone returned to Africa, after another short visit to Bombay, on January 28, 1866, with support from private and public bodies and the status of a British consul at large. His aim, as usual, was the extension of the Gospel and the abolition of the slave trade on the East African coast, but a new object was the exploration of the central African watershed and the possibility of finding the ultimate sources of the Nile River. This time Livingstone went without European subordinates and took only African and Asian followers. Trouble, however, once more broke out among his staff, and Livingstone, prematurely aged from the hardships of his previous expeditions, found it difficult to cope. Striking out from Mikindani on the east coast, he was compelled by Ngoni raids to give up his original intention of avoiding Portuguese territory and reaching the country around Lake Tanganyika by passing north of Lake Nyasa. The expedition was forced south, and in September some of Livingstone's followers deserted him. To avoid punishment when they returned to Zanzibar, they concocted the story that Livingstone had been killed by the Ngoni. Although it was proved the following year that he was alive, a touch of drama was added to the reports circulating abroad about his expedition.

That drama mounted as Livingstone moved north again from the south end of Lake Nyasa. Early in 1867 a deserter carried off his medical chest, but Livingstone pressed on into central Africa. He was the first European to reach Lake Mweru (November 8, 1867) and Lake Bangweulu (July 18, 1868). Assisted by Arab traders, Livingstone reached Lake Tanganyika in

February 1869. Despite illness, he went on and arrived on March 29, 1871, at his ultimate northwesterly point, Nyangwe, on the Lualaba River leading into the Congo River basin. This was farther west than any European had penetrated.

When he returned to Ujiji on the eastern shore of Lake Tanganyika on October 23, 1871, Livingstone was a sick and failing man. Search parties had been sent to look for him because he had not been heard from in several years, and Henry M. Stanley, a correspondent of the *New York Herald*, found the explorer, greeting him with the now famous quote, "Dr. Livingstone, I presume?" (The exact date of the encounter is unclear, as the two men wrote different dates in their journals; Livingstone's journal suggests that the meeting took place sometime in October 24–28, 1871, while Stanley reported November 10.) Stanley brought much-needed food and medicine, and Livingstone soon recovered. He joined Stanley in exploring the northern reaches of Lake Tanganyika and then accompanied him to Unyanyembe, 200 miles (320 km) eastward. But he refused all Stanley's pleas to leave Africa with him, and on March 14, 1872, Stanley departed for England to add, with journalistic fervour, to the saga of David Livingstone.

Livingstone moved south again, obsessed by his quest for the Nile sources and his desire for the destruction of the slave trade, but his illness overcame him. In May 1873, at Chitambo in what is now northern Zambia, Livingstone's African servants found him dead, kneeling by his bedside as if in prayer. In order to embalm Livingstone's body, they removed his heart and viscera and buried them in African soil. In a difficult journey of nine months, they carried his body to the coast. It was taken to England and, in a great Victorian funeral, was buried in Westminster Abbey on April 18, 1874. *The Last Journals of David Livingstone* were published in the same year.

INFLUENCE

In his 30 years of travel and Christian missionary work in southern, central, and eastern Africa—often in places where no European had previously ventured—Livingstone may well have influenced Western attitudes toward Africa more than any other individual before him. His discoveries—geographic, technical, medical, and social—provided a complex body of knowledge that is still being explored. In spite of his paternalism and Victorian prejudices, Livingstone believed wholeheartedly in the African's ability to advance into the modern world. He was, in this sense, a forerunner not only of European imperialism in Africa but also of African nationalism.

LUDWIG LEICHHARDT

(b. October 23, 1813, Trebatsch, Prussia [now in Germany]—d. after April 4, 1848, Australia)

The German-born explorer and naturalist Friedrich Wilhelm Ludwig Leichhardt became one of Australia's earliest heroes. His mysterious disappearance in 1848 aroused efforts to find him or his remains for nearly a century.

While Leichhardt was a student at the universities of Berlin (1831, 1834–36) and Göttingen (1833), he turned from philosophy to natural science. He also met a fellow student from England, William Nicholson, with whom he returned to England in 1837. The two pursued their own course of study: medicine and natural science at the Royal College of Surgeons and the British Museum in London and at the Jardin des Plantes in Paris. They also did field work in England, France, Italy, and Switzerland. In 1841 Nicholson provided Leichhardt with funds and paid his way to Australia.

Leichhardt landed at Sydney in 1842 intent on exploring the interior of Australia. From 1842 to 1844 he did field work in the Hunter River Valley, arranged plant and rock collections, and worked on geological notes, lecturing the while. An official overland expedition had been proposed to the Colonial Office, but Leichhardt impatiently arranged his own with a public subscription. He sailed from Sydney with six companions in August 1844, picked up four more members of the party, and departed from the farthest outpost on Darling Downs in October to cross to Port Essington. Two members turned back and one was killed by Aboriginal people, but the rest reached Port Essington in December 1845. The party had been given up for dead, and their return to Sydney was greeted with the greatest astonishment and joy. They received a large government grant and an even larger amount in private subscriptions. Leichhardt's journal of the expedition was published in 1847.

The second expedition, a party of eight, set out in December 1846 to cross from Darling Downs to the west coast and south to the Swan River settlement. Forced back by loss of animals taken for food and by fever, the party set out again in June 1847 but again had to return. Leichhardt organized a party of six others and set out in March 1848, but the party was never heard of after leaving a point near the present town of Roma, from which he had written his last letter, dated April 4. Leichhardt had expected the expedition to take two years. Search for the party began

Ludwig Leichhardt. Universal Images Group/Getty Images

in 1852 and continued into the 1930s, spurred on in its latest stages by rumours of white men living among the Aboriginals. Many of the searching parties brought back valuable information for later settlement.

Leichhardt's expeditions discovered extensive areas suitable for settlement and many important streams and provided an early map. His early success was rewarded by a share of the 1847 prize of the Geographical Society of Paris and by the Patron's medal of the Royal Geographical Society of London. Prussia forgave him his failure to perform his military service. Records of his scientific work and his lectures were published worldwide.

His legend provided the basis for the hero of Patrick White's novel *Voss* (1957). Leichhardt's letters (3 vol.) were published in 1968.

EDWARD JOHN EYRE

(b. August 5, 1815, Hornsea, Yorkshire, England—d. November 30, 1901, near Tavistock, Devon)

Edward John Eyre was the English explorer of Australia for whom Lake Eyre and the Eyre Peninsula (both in South Australia) are named. He was subsequently a British colonial official in Australia and elsewhere.

Emigrating from England for reasons of health, Eyre reached Australia in March 1833. As a sheep farmer he became a pioneer "overlander," driving stock from Sydney to Adelaide. He explored the desert northwest of Adelaide and then (June 1840–July 1841) made an extremely hazard-ous journey around the Great Australian Bight. For several years he served as a magistrate and protector of Aboriginal peoples, whose language and customs he learned.

After leaving Australia in 1845, Eyre was lieutenant gov-ernor of New Zealand (1846–53) and of St. Vincent, in the West Indies (1854–60). His service as acting governor of the Leeward Islands (1860–61) and of Jamaica (1861–64) was rewarded with his permanent appointment as gov-ernor of Jamaica. On October 11, 1865, a revolt by blacks began at Morant Bay, and, in the repression that followed, the total of executions passed 400. Eyre then caused the island's legislature to abolish itself and the Jamaican con-stitution (January 17, 1866), whereupon Jamaica became a crown colony. After both commending Eyre for crush-ing the rebellion and censuring him for taking excessive reprisals, the British government recalled him in July 1866. Eyre's behaviour sparked an intense controversy among prominent British intellectuals; John Stuart Mill, Herbert Spencer, and Thomas Henry Huxley advocated his trial for murder, while his side was taken by Thomas Carlyle, John Ruskin, and Alfred, Lord Tennyson. A grand jury in London declined to indict him for murder (June 1868), and he was acquitted in a civil case brought against him by a Jamaican.

SIR JOSEPH DALTON HOOKER

(b. June 30, 1817, Halesworth, Suffolk, England—d. December 10, 1911, Sunningdale, Berkshire)

The English botanist Sir Joseph Dalton Hooker was noted for his botanical travels and studies and for his encouragement of Charles Darwin and of Darwin's theories. The younger son of Sir William Jackson Hooker, he was assistant director of the Royal Botanic Gardens at Kew from 1855 to 1865 and, succeeding his father, was then director from 1865 to 1885.

Hooker, unlike his father, had the benefit of a formal education and was graduated from the University of Glasgow with an M.D., in 1839. Through his familiarity with his father's herbarium, he was well prepared for the first of his many travels—as surgeon-botanist aboard HMS *Erebus* on the Antarctic expedition of 1839–43. Thereafter, a steady stream of publications followed, punctuated by his own travels: *The Botany of the Antarctic Voyage of H.M. Discovery-Ships* Erebus *and* Terror *in 1839–1843* (1844–60); *Rhododendrons of Sikkim Himalya* (1849); *The Flora of British India* (1872–97); *Handbook of the New Zealand Flora* (1864); and *Journal of a Tour in Marocco and the Great Atlas* (1878). His last major botanical expedition, to the Rocky Mountains and California (1877), led to the publication of several important papers concerning the relationship of American and Asian floras. His travels resulted in the discovery of species new to science, many of which were soon introduced to horticultural circles. Even more important, however, were the data, which gained him an international reputation as a plant geographer.

In 1851 Joseph Hooker married Frances Henslow, the daughter of a botanist. Six children survived her death in 1874. By his second wife, Hyacinth Symonds Jardine, whom he married in 1876, he had two sons. He became assistant director of Kew in 1855, a position he retained until 1865, when he succeeded his father as director, serving in that capacity until his own retirement in 1885. Many honours came to Hooker, including the presidency of

Sir Joseph Dalton Hooker. Universal Images Group/ Getty Images

SIR FRANCIS LEOPOLD MCCLINTOCK

the Royal Society (1872–77) and a knighthood (1877). He remained active until shortly before his death.

One of the most significant results of his travels was an attempt to explain the geographical distribution of plants and their seemingly anomalous variations. As a close friend of Charles Darwin and one well acquainted with the latter's early work, Hooker, along with the geologist Sir Charles Lyell, presided at the historic meeting of the Linnean Society (London) in July 1858. It was their function to adjudicate the priority claims concerning natural selection as the mechanism for evolution, which had been advanced simultaneously by Darwin and Alfred Russel Wallace. By lending his support to a scientific claim that was soon to be attacked on extrascientific grounds, Hooker was among the first to demonstrate the importance and applicability of the evolutionary theory to botany in general and to plant geography in particular. The capstone to Hooker's career came in 1883 with the publication of the final volume of the *Genera Plantarum*, written in conjunction with the British botanist George Bentham, who had helped establish vascular plant taxonomy. This world flora, describing 7,569 genera and approximately 97,000 species of seed-bearing plants, was based on a personal examination of the specimens cited, the vast majority of which were deposited at Kew.

SIR FRANCIS LEOPOLD MCCLINTOCK

(b. July 8, 1819, Dundalk, County Louth, Ireland—d. November 17, 1907, London, England)

Sir Francis Leopold McClintock was the British naval officer and explorer who discovered the tragic fate of the British explorer Sir John Franklin and his 1845 expedition to the North American Arctic. Before his own successful search of 1857–59, McClintock took part in three earlier efforts to find Franklin. On the second and third of these (1850–51 and 1852–54), his improvements in the planning and execution of sledge journeys greatly advanced the possibilities of Arctic exploration.

The first information suggesting that Franklin's party had perished around King William Island, now in Canada's Northwest Territories, was obtained from Inuit (Eskimos) in 1854. When the British government refused to equip another search expedition, Franklin's widow equipped the *Fox*, with McClintock in command. He found the graves of some of Franklin's crew as well as remains from Franklin's ships and some of his belongings. He also received an old Eskimo woman's account of how Franklin's starving men died in their tracks as they sought to journey southward on foot. The most important evidence that McClintock recovered was a written record of Franklin's expedition up to April 25, 1848. McClintock's account of his journey, *The Voyage of the "Fox" in the Arctic Seas: A Narrative of the Fate of Sir John Franklin and His Companions*, was published in 1859, and he was knighted in 1860.

JOHANNES REBMANN

(b. January 16, 1820, Gerlingen, Württemberg [Germany]—d. October 4, 1876, Korntal, near Stuttgart [Germany])

The German missionary and explorer Johannes Rebmann was the first European to penetrate Africa from its Indian Ocean coast. Rebmann and his associate, Johann Ludwig Krapf, also were the discoverers of Kilimanjaro (Africa's highest point) and Mount Kenya and paved the way for the great East African explorations of the Britons Sir Richard Burton, John Hanning Speke, and David Livingstone.

Rebmann arrived in East Africa in 1846 and began missionary work among the coastal tribes. Though he felt he was only incidentally an explorer, he began expeditions into the interior and, in May 1848, was the first European to see Kilimanjaro. Krapf first sighted Mount Kenya in December 1849. At first the existence of these mountains was not believed in Europe, but Rebmann's accounts, together with his sketch map of an enormous lake (Nyasa) in the interior, stimulated scientific exploration of the sources and drainage system of the Nile River.

ROBERT O'HARA BURKE

(b. May 6?, 1820/21, St. Clerah's, County Galway, Ireland—d. June 28?, 1861, Australia)

The Irish-born explorer Robert O'Hara Burke led the first expedition known to attempt the crossing of Australia from south to north.

Sponsored by the Royal Society of Victoria, Burke left Melbourne with a party of 18 in August 1860. The plan was to establish bases from which an advance party would leave

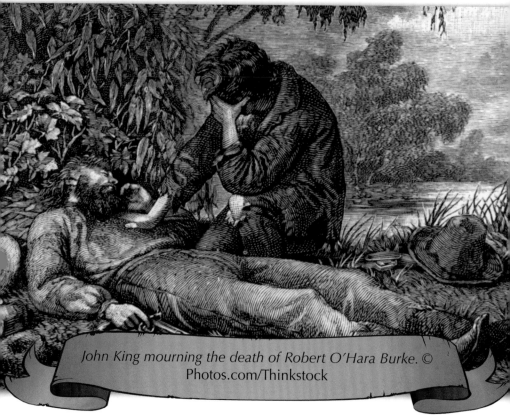

John King mourning the death of Robert O'Hara Burke. ©
Photos.com/Thinkstock

to prepare for those with bulkier supplies. But about midway, at Barcoo Creek (now Cooper Creek in eastern South Australia), the impatient Burke decided to make the rest of the trip accompanied only by his second in command, William John Wills, and by Charles Gray and John King. The four reached northern Australia in February 1861 but could not penetrate the swamps and jungle scrub that lay between them and the Gulf of Carpentaria.

Gray died of exhaustion on the return trip. On arriving at the Barcoo camp, Burke found it deserted. The rear party, instructed to remain three months, had waited for more than four, but it had left the morning of the same day on which Burke, Wills, and King returned. Food sufficient to get them to the nearest town was left at a marked spot, but Burke and King imprudently decided to head for Adelaide on the southern coast. Burke died two days later of exhaustion. King, who returned to camp and found Wills dead, was eventually rescued by a search party. A statue to Burke and King was erected in Melbourne. Wills's journal, found with his body, is an account of the venture.

HEINRICH BARTH

(b. February 16, 1821, Hamburg [Germany]—
d. November 25, 1865, Berlin, Prussia [Germany])

The German geographer Heinrich Barth was one of the great explorers of Africa. Educated in the classics at the University of Berlin, Barth was a competent linguist who was fluent in French, Spanish, Italian, English, and Arabic. He traveled the Mediterranean coastal areas that are now part of Tunisia and Libya (1845–47) and published his observations in 1849.

Early in 1850, with the explorer James Richardson and the geologist and astronomer Adolf Overweg, he set out from Tripoli (Libya) across the Sahara on a British-sponsored expedition to the western Sudan (a term then in use for most of central West Africa). When Richardson died a year later in what is now northern Nigeria, Barth assumed command. He explored the area south and southeast of Lake Chad and mapped the upper reaches of the Benue River. Overweg died in September 1852, and Barth traveled to the city of Timbuktu, now in Mali. He remained there for six months before returning, via Tripoli, to London (1855).

Despite ill health and the loss of his colleagues, Barth had traveled some 10,000 miles (16,000 km), laid down accurate routes by dead reckoning, and returned to Europe with the first account of the middle section of the Niger River. His four large volumes, *Reisen und Entdeckungen in Nord- und Central-Afrika in den Jahren 1849 bis 1855* (1857–58; "Travels and Discoveries in North and Central Africa in the Years 1849–1855"), remain one of the most comprehensive works on the area and contain an immense amount of anthropological, historical, and linguistic information as well as the daily travel details he so assiduously recorded. His work was honoured and rewarded financially by the British government. Later travels took him to Turkey and Asia Minor as well as to Spain, Italy, and the Alps. He was appointed professor of geography at the University of Berlin (1863).

SIR RICHARD BURTON

(b. March 19, 1821, Torquay, Devonshire, England—d. October 20, 1890, Trieste, Austria-Hungary [now in Italy])

The remarkable English scholar-explorer and Orientalist Sir Richard Francis Burton was the first European to discover Lake Tanganyika and to penetrate hitherto-forbidden Muslim cities. He published 43 volumes on his explorations and almost 30 volumes of translations, including an unexpurgated translation of *The Arabian Nights*.

Richard Burton, c. 1880. Hulton Archive/Getty Images

EARLY LIFE AND CAREER

Burton was of mixed English, Irish, and possibly French ancestry. His father, retiring early from an unsuccessful army career, chose to raise his two sons and daughter in France and Italy, where young Richard developed his astonishing talent for languages to such an extent that before matriculating at Trinity College, Oxford, in 1840, he had become fluent in French, Italian, and the Béarnais and Neapolitan dialects, as well as in Greek and Latin. His continental upbringing, however, left him ambivalent about his national identity. He called himself "a waif, a stray...a blaze of light, without a focus," and complained that "England is the only country where I never feel at home."

Expelled from Oxford in 1842 because of a minor breach of discipline, he went to India as subaltern officer in the 18th Regiment of Bombay Native Infantry during England's war with the Sindh (now a province of Pakistan). He mastered Arabic and Hindī and during his eight-year stay became proficient also in Marathi, Sindhi, Punjabi, Telugu, Pashto, and Multani. Eventually in his travels over the world he learned 25 languages, with dialects that brought the number to 40.

As a favoured intelligence officer of Sir Charles James Napier, commander of the English forces in the Sindh, Captain Burton went in disguise as a Muslim merchant in the bazaars, bringing back detailed reports. Napier in 1845 asked him to investigate the homosexual brothels in Karachi; his explicit study resulted in their destruction; it also resulted, after Napier's departure, in the destruction of Burton's promising career, when the report was forwarded to Bombay (now Mumbai) by an unfriendly officer who hoped to see Burton dismissed in disgrace.

Though the effort failed, Burton realized his reputation was irreparably clouded and returned, ill and disconsolate, to England.

From his 29th to his 32nd year he lived with his mother and sister in Boulogne, France, where he wrote four books on India, including *Sindh, and the Races That Inhabit the Valley of the Indus* (1851), a brilliant ethnological study, published before the new science of ethnology had a proper tradition against which its merits could be evaluated. Meanwhile he perfected his long-cherished plans for going to Mecca.

EXPLORATION IN ARABIA

Disguising himself as a Pashtun, an Afghan Muslim, in 1853 he went to Cairo, Suez, and Medina and then traveled the bandit-ridden route to the sacred city of Mecca, where at great risk he measured and sketched the mosque and holy Muslim shrine, the Ka'bah. Though not the first non-Muslim to penetrate and describe the "mother of cities," Burton was the most sophisticated and the most accurate. His *Pilgrimage to El-Medinah and Mecca* (1855–56) was not only a great adventure narrative but also a classic commentary on Muslim life and manners, especially on the annual pilgrimage. Instead of returning to London to enjoy his sudden fame, however, he organized a new expedition in 1854 to the equally forbidden East African city of Harar (Harer) and became the first European to enter this Muslim citadel without being executed. He described his adventures in *First Footsteps in East Africa* (1856).

By this time Burton had become fascinated by the idea of discovering the source of the White Nile and in 1855 planned an expedition with three officers of the British East India Company, including John Hanning Speke, intending to push across Somaliland. Africans attacked the party near Berbera, however, killing one member of the party and seriously wounding Speke. Burton himself had a javelin hurled through his jaw and was forced to return to England. After recovery, in July 1855, he went to the Crimea to volunteer in the war against Russia. At the Dardanelles he helped train Turkish irregulars but saw no action at the front.

The Crimean War over, he turned again to the Nile search, leading an expedition inland from Zanzibar with John Speke in 1857–58. They suffered almost every kind of hardship Africa could inflict. When they finally arrived on the shores of Lake Tanganyika, Burton was so ill from malaria he could not walk, and Speke was virtually blind. Ailing, and disappointed by native information that the Rusizi River to the north poured into rather than out of the lake, Burton wished to return and prepare a new expedition. Speke, however, who had recovered more quickly, pushed on alone to the northeast and discovered Lake Victoria, which he was convinced was the true Nile source. Burton's unwillingness to accept this theory without further exploration led to quarrels with Speke and their eventual estrangement.

Speke was the first to return to London, where he was lionized and given funds to return to Africa. Burton, largely ignored and denied financing for a new exploration of his own, felt betrayed. His *Lake Regions of Central Africa* (1860) attacked Speke's claims and exacerbated their by then public feud.

In 1860 Burton went off unexpectedly to the United States, where he traveled by stagecoach to the Mormon capital, Salt Lake City. The resulting volume, *City of the Saints* (1861), showed that he could write with sophistication about the nature of the Mormon church, compose a vivid portrait of its leader, Brigham Young, and also be dispassionate about the Mormon practice of polygamy, which was then outraging most Americans. Shortly after his return from the United States, in January 1861, he and Isabel Arundell, the daughter of an aristocratic family, whom he had been courting since 1856, were married secretly.

FOREIGN OFFICE

Burton now entered the British Foreign Office as consul in Fernando Po, a Spanish island off the coast of West Africa (now Bioko, Equatorial Guinea). During his three years there, he made many short trips of exploration into West Africa, gathering enough material to fill five books. His explicit descriptions of tribal rituals concerning birth, marriage, and death, as well as fetishism, ritual murder, cannibalism, and bizarre sexual practices, though admired by modern anthropologists, won him no favour with the Foreign Office, which considered him eccentric if not dangerous.

Returning to London on leave in September 1864, Burton was invited to debate with Speke before the British Association for the Advancement of Science. Speke, who with the British soldier and explorer James Augustus Grant had made a memorable journey from Zanzibar to Lake Victoria and then down the whole length of the Nile, was expected to defend his conviction that Lake Victoria was the true Nile source. After the preliminary session on September 15, Speke went hunting, dying mysteriously as a result of a shotgun wound in his chest. The coroner's jury ruled the death an accident, but Burton believed it to be a suicide. He wrote in anguish to a friend, "The charitable say that he shot himself, the uncharitable say that I shot him."

Burton spent the next four years as consul in Santos, Brazil, where he wrote a book on the Brazilian Highlands (1869) and translated *Vikram and the Vampire, or Tales of Hindu Devilry* (1870). He also began translating the works of the romantic Portuguese poet-explorer Luís de Camões, with whom he felt a deep sense of kinship. Yet his work did not help him to overcome his increasing aversion for Brazil. He took to drink, and finally he sent his devoted wife to London to obtain a better post for him. She succeeded in persuading the Foreign Secretary to appoint Burton consul in Damascus (Syria).

Back in the Middle East, which he loved, Burton for a time was highly successful as a diplomat; but Muslim intrigue, complicated by the proselytizing indiscretions of his Roman Catholic wife, resulted in his humiliating dismissal in August 1871. The details of this event were recorded by Isabel Burton in her lively, defensive *Inner Life of Syria* (1875).

TRIESTE

In 1872 Burton reluctantly accepted the consulate at Trieste (now in Italy), and although he considered it an ignominious exile, he eventually came to cherish it as his home. There he stayed until his death, publishing an astonishing variety of books. He wrote a book on Iceland, one on Etruscan Bologna (reflecting his passion for archaeology), a nostalgic volume on the Sindh, two books on the gold mines of the Midian, and one on the African Gold Coast (now Ghana), none of which matched the great narratives of his earlier adventures. His *Book of the Sword* (1884), a dazzling piece of historical erudition, brought him no more financial success than any of the others. In 1880 he published his best original poetry, *The Kasidah*, written under a pseudonym and patterned after the Rubáiyát of Omar Khayyám.

In Trieste, Burton emerged as a translator of extraordinary virtuosity. He translated and annotated six volumes of Camões, a volume of Neapolitan Italian tales by the Neapolitan soldier, administrator, and writer Giambattista Basile, Il Pentamerone, and Latin poems by the 1st-century BCE Roman writer Catullus. What excited him most, however, was the erotica of the East. Taking it upon himself to introduce to the West the sexual wisdom of the ancient Eastern manuals on the art of love, he risked prosecution and imprisonment to translate and print secretly the *Kama Sutra of Vatsyayana* (1883), *Ananga Ranga* (1885), and *The Perfumed Garden of the Cheikh Nefzaoui* (1886). He also published openly, but privately, an unexpurgated 16-volume edition of the *Arabian Nights* (1885–88), the translation of which was exceptional for its fidelity, vigour, and literary skill. Moreover, he larded these volumes with ethnological footnotes and daring essays on pornography, homosexuality, and the sexual education of women. He railed against the "immodest modesty," the cant, and hypocrisy of his era, displaying psychological insights that anticipated both Havelock Ellis and Sigmund Freud. His *Nights* were praised by some for their robustness and honesty but attacked by others as "garbage of the brothels," "an appalling collection of degrading customs and statistics of vice."

In February 1886 Burton won belated recognition for his services to the crown when Queen Victoria made him Knight Commander of St. Michael and St. George. He died in Trieste four years later. His wife, fearful lest her husband be thought vicious because he collected data on what Victorian England called vice, at once burned the projected new edition of *The Perfumed Garden* he had been annotating. She then wrote a biography of Burton in which she tried to fashion this Rabelaisian scholar-adventurer into a good Catholic, a faithful husband, and a refined and modest man. Afterward she burned almost all of his 40-year collection of diaries and journals. The loss to history and anthropology was monumental; the loss to Burton's biographers, irreparable.

SIR SAMUEL WHITE BAKER

(b. June 8, 1821, London, England—
d. December 30, 1893, Sanford Orleigh, Devon)

S ir Samuel White Baker was the English explorer who, with John Hanning Speke, helped to locate the sources of the Nile River.

The son of a merchant, Baker lived on the Indian Ocean island of Mauritius (1843–45) and in Ceylon (1846–55; now Sri Lanka) before traveling through the Middle East (1856–60). In 1861, with Florence von Sass (who later became his second wife), he went to Africa and for about a year explored the Nile tributaries around the Sudan and Ethiopia border. Using maps supplied by Speke, the Baker expedition set out in February 1863 to find the source of the Nile. In March 1864 Baker determined the source to be a lake lying between modern Uganda and Congo (Kinshasa), which he named Albert Nyanza (Lake Albert) for Queen Victoria's consort. He was knighted in 1866, the year after he returned to England.

In 1869 the Ottoman viceroy of Egypt, Ismā'īl Pasha, asked Baker to command a military expedition to the

Nile equatorial regions. There the explorer helped to put down the slave trade and annexed territories of which he was appointed governor general for four years. His books include *The Rifle and the Hound in Ceylon* (1854) and *The Nile Tributaries of Abyssinia* (1867).

CHARLES FRANCIS HALL

(b. 1821, Rochester, New Hampshire, U.S.—
d. November 8, 1871, Thank God Harbor,
Greenland)

The American explorer Charles Francis Hall made three Arctic expeditions.

Hall spent his early life in Ohio, where he held such various jobs as those of blacksmith, journalist, stationer, and engraver, before taking an interest in exploration. In 1860 he landed alone from a whaleboat at Frobisher Bay on the southern end of Baffin Island (now in the Northwest Territories, Canada) and spent two years exploring in the bay area, which the English navigator Martin Frobisher had reached in 1578. Hall's purpose was to locate survivors from Sir John Franklin's expedition of 1845, but, though he did not succeed in this endeavour, he did find many remains from Frobisher's expedition. After returning home (1862), he wrote *Arctic Researches, and Life among the Esquimaux* (1865).

In 1864 Hall returned again to search for survivors from Franklin's voyage. From the north end of Hudson Bay, he began five years and 3,000 miles (4,830 km) of journeying by sledge, in the course of which he learned much about the fate of Franklin's expedition and found a number of relics of the party.

His final venture was to command a U.S. government-sponsored expedition attempting to reach the North Pole. On June 29, 1871, he sailed from New York City aboard the naval steamer *Polaris*. Hall passed through the Kennedy and Robeson channels, which separate northwestern Greenland from the northeastern Canadian Arctic, charted both coasts, and reached 82°11' N, then the northernmost limit of exploration by a ship. The Polaris turned southward and anchored off Greenland at 81°37' N. From a land base, Hall sledged to 83° N but died suddenly on the return trip.

HEINRICH SCHLIEMANN

(b. January 6, 1822, Neubukow, Mecklenburg-Schwerin [Germany]—d. December 26, 1890, Naples [Italy])

Heinrich Schliemann was a German archaeologist and the excavator of Troy, Mycenae, and Tiryns; he is often considered to be the modern discoverer of pre-historic Greece.

YOUTH AND EARLY CAREER

Schliemann was the son of a poor pastor. A picture of Troy in flames in a history book his father had given him when he was seven years old remained in his memory throughout his life and sustained his fervent belief in the historical foundations of the Homeric poems. At the age of 14 he was apprenticed to a grocer, and it was in the grocer's shop that he heard Homer declaimed in the original Greek. After several years in the shop, ill health forced him to leave, and he became a cabin boy on a ship bound from Hamburg to Venezuela. After the vessel was wrecked off the Dutch coast, he became office boy and then bookkeeper for a trading firm in Amsterdam. He had a passion and a flair for languages, as well as a remarkable memory; these factors, combined with great energy and determination, enabled him to learn to read and write fluently between 8 and 13 languages—accounts vary, but his competence certainly included Russian and both ancient and modern Greek.

In 1846 his firm sent him to St. Petersburg, Russia, as an agent. There he founded a business on his own and embarked, among other things, on the indigo trade. In 1852 he married Ekaterina Lyschin. He made a fortune at the time of the Crimean War, mainly as a military contractor. In the 1850s he was in the United States and became a U.S. citizen, retaining this nationality for the rest of his life. Returning to Russia he retired from business at the age of 36 and began to devote his energies and money to the study of prehistoric archaeology, particularly the problem of identifying the site of Homeric Troy. To train himself, he traveled extensively in Greece, Italy, Scandinavia, Germany, and Syria and then went around the world, visiting India, China, and Japan (he wrote a book about the last two countries). He also studied archaeology in Paris.

In 1868 Schliemann took his large fortune to Greece, visiting Homeric sites there and in Asia Minor (modern Turkey), and the following year he published his first book, *Ithaka, der Peloponnes und Troja* ("Ithaca, the

Peloponnese, and Troy"). In this work he argued that Hisarlık, in Asia Minor, and not Bunarbashi, a short distance south of it, was the site of Troy and that the graves of the Greek commander Agamemnon and his wife, Clytemnestra, at Mycenae, described by the Greek geographer Pausanias, were not the *tholoi* (vaulted tombs) outside the citadel walls but lay inside the citadel. He was able to prove both theories by excavation in the course of the next few years. He had divorced his Russian wife, Ekaterina, and in 1869 married someone decades younger than he, a Greek teenager named Sophia Engastromenos, whom he had selected through a marriage bureau.

DISCOVERY OF TROY

Although some isolated discoveries had been made before he began digging, Schliemann has rightly been called the creator of prehistoric Greek archaeology. The French geologist Ferdinand Fouqué dug on the island of Thera (Santoríni) in 1862 and found fresco-covered walls of houses and painted pottery beneath 26 feet (8 metres) of pumice, the result of the great eruption that divided the original island into Thera (modern Greek Thíra) and two small islets to the west. Geologists at that time dated the Thera eruption to 2000 BCE (subsequently adjusted to between about 1620 and 1500 BCE), which suggested a great antiquity for Fouqué's finds and the existence of prehistoric cultures hitherto unknown in the Aegean. The English archaeologist Frederick Calvert had dug at Hisarlık, and in 1871 Schliemann took up his work at this large man-made mound. He believed that the Homeric Troy must be in the lowest level of the mound, and he dug uncritically through the upper levels. In 1873 he uncovered fortifications and the remains of a city of great antiquity, and he discovered a treasure of gold jewelry, which he smuggled out of Turkey. He believed the city he had found was Homeric Troy and identified the treasure as that of Priam. His discoveries and theories, first published in *Trojanische Altertümer* (1874; "Trojan Antiquity"), were received skeptically by many scholars, but others, including the prime minister of England, William Ewart Gladstone, himself a classical scholar, and a wide public, accepted his identification.

When he proposed to resume work at Hisarlık in February 1874, he was delayed by a lawsuit with the Ottoman government about the division of his spoils, particularly the gold treasure, and it was not until April 1876 that he obtained permission to resume work. In 1874–76 Schliemann dug instead at the site of the Treasury of Minyas, at Orchomenus in Boeotia (a region of Greece northwest of Athens), but found little except the remains of a beautiful ceiling. During this delay he also published *Troja und seine Ruinen* (1875; "Troy and Its Ruins") and began excavation at Mycenae. In August 1876, he began work in the tholoi, digging by the Lion Gate and then inside the citadel walls, where he found a double ring of slabs and, within that ring, five shaft graves (a sixth was found immediately after his departure). Buried with 16 bodies in this circle of shaft graves was a large treasure of gold, silver, bronze, and ivory objects. Schliemann had hoped to find—and believed he had found—the tombs of Agamemnon and Clytemnestra, and he published his finds in his Mykenä (1878; "Mycenae").

After an unsuccessful excavation in Ithaca in 1878, he resumed work at Hisarlık the same year. He conducted a third excavation at Troy in 1882–83 and a fourth from 1888 until his death. In his first season he had worked alone with his wife, Sophia. In 1879 he was assisted by Emile Burnouf, a classical archaeologist, and by Rudolf Virchow, the famous German pathologist, who was also the founder of the German Society for Anthropology, Ethnology, and Prehistory. In his last two seasons Schliemann had the expert assistance of Wilhelm Dörpfeld, who had trained as an architect and had worked at the German excavations at Olympia. Dörpfeld brought to Troy the new system and efficiency of the German classical archaeologists working in Greece, and he was able to expose the stratigraphy at Troy more clearly than before and to revolutionize Schliemann's techniques. In 1884, Schliemann, together with Dörpfeld, excavated the great fortified site of Tiryns near Mycenae.

Toward the end of his life, Schliemann suffered greatly with ear trouble and traveled in Europe, visiting specialists and hoping for a cure. None was forthcoming. In great pain and alone, on December 25, 1890, while walking across a square in Naples, he collapsed; he died the next day.

ASSESSMENT

Schliemann's work of discovery in archaeology is easy to assess. He discovered Homeric Troy as well as a city that existed long before Homer—a prehistoric Bronze Age civilization in Turkey; this was also what he discovered at Mycenae. Hitherto, ancient historians had thought of four empires: Greece, Rome, Egypt, and Babylon-Assyria; Schliemann discovered two new civilizations and enormously lengthened the perspective of history. He nearly discovered a third, namely that of prehistoric Crete.

He had long thought that there must have existed in the Mediterranean a civilization earlier than Mycenae and Bronze Age Hisarlık, and he guessed that it might be in

Crete. At one time he contemplated excavation in Crete, but he could not agree to the price asked for the land; thus, the discovery of the pre-Mycenean civilization of Minoan Crete was left to Sir Arthur Evans 10 years after Schliemann's death.

Schliemann was one of the first popularizers of archaeology. With his books and his dispatches to *The Times*, the *Daily Telegraph*, and other papers he kept the world informed and excited by his archaeological discoveries as no one previously had been able to do. It has been said that "every person of culture and education lived through the drama of discovering Troy." Schliemann became a symbol not only of the new archaeological scholarship of the second half of the 19th century but also of the romance and excitement of archaeology. Scholars and the public were inspired by him, and when he died Sir John Myres, Camden Professor of Ancient History at the University of Oxford, said that to many it seemed that "the spring had gone out of the year."

When Schliemann began excavating, no corpus of accepted practice existed for archaeological fieldwork. Like Sir Flinders Petrie and Augustus Pitt-Rivers, he was a pioneer. Stratigraphy had been observed and understood in the Danish peat bogs, the Jutland barrows, and the prehistoric Swiss lake dwellings, but Hisarlık was the first large dry-land man-made mound to be dug. It is not surprising that Schliemann was at first puzzled by what he found, but, eventually, with the assistance of Dörpfeld, he was able to untangle the stratigraphy. There was a wide variation in the assessment of his technique as an excavator. He did extremely well for someone starting to dig in the 1870s, yet he was often unfairly criticized by those who were excavating similar mounds in the Middle East 100 years later.

ADOLF OVERWEG

(b. July 24, 1822, Hamburg [Germany]—
d. September 27, 1852, Maduari, Chad)

The German geologist, astronomer, and traveler Adolf Overweg was the first European to circumnavigate and map Lake Chad. Overweg was also a member of a pioneering mission to open the Central African interior to regular trade routes from the north coast of the continent.

In 1849 Overweg joined an expedition, headed by the English explorer James Richardson, which was mounted by the British government for the purpose of opening commercial relations with the kingdoms of Central Africa. The expedition left Tripoli, in Libya, in the spring of 1850 and crossed the Sahara southward. Early in 1851 the group split up, and Overweg went on alone by way of Zinder (in present south-central Niger) to Kukawa (northeastern Nigeria), where he joined Heinrich Barth, the expedition's scientist (and, after the death of Richardson, its leader). The two spent 18 months exploring southward to Adamawa emirate (Nigeria) and the Benue River, around Lake Chad and to the southeast, until Overweg's death.

ALFRED RUSSEL WALLACE

(b. January 8, 1823, Usk, Monmouthshire,
Wales—d. November 7, 1913, Broadstone,
Dorset, England)

Alfred Russel (A.R.) Wallace was a renowned British humanist, naturalist, geographer, and social critic. He became a public figure in England during the second half of the 19th century, known for his courageous views on scientific, social, and spiritualist subjects. His formulation of the theory of evolution by natural selection, which predated Charles Darwin's published contributions, is his most outstanding legacy, but it was just one of many controversial issues he studied and wrote about during his lifetime. Wallace's wide-ranging interests—from socialism to spiritualism, from island biogeography to life on Mars, from evolution to land nationalization—stemmed from his profound concern with the moral, social, and political values of human life.

EARLY LIFE AND WORK

The eighth of nine children born to Thomas Vere Wallace and Mary Anne Greenell, Alfred Russel Wallace grew up in modest circumstances in rural Wales and then in Hertford, Hertfordshire, England. His formal education was limited to six years at the one-room Hertford Grammar School. Although his education was curtailed by the family's

Alfred Russel Wallace, c. 1894. Hulton Archive/Getty Images

worsening financial situation, his home was a rich source of books, maps, and gardening activities, which Wallace remembered as enduring sources of learning and pleasure. Wallace's parents belonged to the Church of England, and as a child Wallace attended services. His lack of enthusiasm for organized religion became more pronounced when he was exposed to secular teachings at a London mechanics' institute, the "Hall of Science" off Tottenham Court Road. Living in London with his brother John, an apprentice carpenter, the 14-year-old Wallace became familiar with the lives of tradesmen and labourers, and he shared in their efforts at self-education. Here Wallace read treatises and attended lectures by Robert Owen and his son Robert Dale Owen that formed the basis of his religious skepticism and his reformist and socialist political philosophy.

In 1837 Wallace became an apprentice in the surveying business of his eldest brother, William. New tax laws (Tithe Commutation Act, 1836) and the division of public land among landowners (General Enclosures Act, 1845) created a demand for accurate surveys and maps of farmlands, public lands, and parishes, as surveys and maps made according to regulations were legal documents in executing these laws. For approximately 8 of the next 10 years, Wallace surveyed and mapped in Bedfordshire and then in Wales. He lived among farmers and artisans and saw the injustices suffered by the poor as a result of the new laws. Wallace's detailed observations of their habits are recorded in one of his first writing efforts, an essay on "the South Wales Farmer," which is reproduced in his autobiography. When surveying work could not be found as a result of violent uprisings by the Welsh farmers, Wallace spent a year (1844) teaching at a boys' school, the Collegiate School in Leicester, Leicestershire, England. After his brother William died in early 1845, Wallace worked in London and Wales, saw to his brother's business, surveyed for a proposed railway line, and built a mechanics' institute at Neath, Wales, with his brother John.

THE CAREER OF A NATURALIST

As a surveyor, Wallace spent a great deal of time outdoors, both for work and pleasure. An enthusiastic amateur naturalist with an intellectual bent, he read widely in natural history, history, and political economy, including works by Charles Darwin, Alexander von Humboldt, English zoologist and botanist William Swainson, and English economist and demographer Thomas Malthus. He also read works and attended lectures on phrenology and mesmerism, forming an interest in nonmaterial mental phenomena that grew increasingly prominent later in his life. Inspired by reading about organic evolution in Robert Chambers's controversial *Vestiges of the Natural History of Creation* (1844), unemployed, and ardent in his love of nature, Wallace and his naturalist friend Henry Walter Bates, who had introduced Wallace to entomology four years earlier, traveled to Brazil in 1848 as self-employed specimen collectors. Wallace and Bates participated in the culture of natural history collecting, honing practical skills to identify, collect, and send back to England biological objects that were highly valued in the flourishing trade in natural specimens. The two young men amicably parted ways after several joint collecting ventures; Bates spent 11 years in the region, while Wallace spent a total of four years traveling, collecting, mapping, drawing, and writing in unexplored regions of the Amazon River basin. He studied the languages and habits of the peoples he encountered; he collected butterflies, other insects, and birds; and he searched for clues to solve the mystery of the

origin of plant and animal species. Except for one ship-
ment of specimens sent to his agent in London, however,
most of Wallace's collections were lost on his voyage home
when his ship went up in flames and sank. Nevertheless, he
managed to save some of his notes before his rescue and
return journey. From these he published several scientific
articles, two books (*Palm Trees of the Amazon and Their Uses*
and *Narrative of Travels on the Amazon and Rio Negro*, both
1853), and a map depicting the course of the Negro River.
These won him acclaim from the Royal Geographical
Society, which helped to fund his next collecting venture,
in the Malay Archipelago.

Wallace spent eight years in the Malay Archipelago,
from 1854 to 1862, traveling among the islands, collecting biological specimens for his own research and for
sale, and writing scores of scientific articles on mostly
zoological subjects. Among these were two extraordinary
articles dealing with the origin of new species. The first
of these, published in 1855, concluded with the assertion
that "every species has come into existence coincident
both in space and time with a pre-existing closely allied
species." Wallace then proposed that new species arise
by the progression and continued divergence of varieties
that outlive the parent species in the struggle for existence. In early 1858 he sent a paper outlining these ideas
to Darwin, who saw such a striking coincidence to his
own theory that he consulted his closest colleagues, the
geologist Charles Lyell and the botanist Joseph Dalton
Hooker. The three men decided to present two extracts
of Darwin's previous writings, along with Wallace's paper,
to the Linnean Society. The resulting set of papers, with
both Darwin's and Wallace's names, was published as
a single article entitled "On the Tendency of Species to
Form Varieties; and on the Perpetuation of Varieties and
Species by Natural Means of Selection" in the *Proceedings*

of the Linnean Society in 1858. This compromise sought to avoid a conflict of priority interests and was reached without Wallace's knowledge. Wallace's research on the geographic distribution of animals among the islands of the Malay Archipelago provided crucial evidence for his evolutionary theories and led him to devise what soon became known as Wallace's Line, the boundary that separates the fauna of Australia from that of Asia.

Wallace returned to England in 1862 an established natural scientist and geographer, as well as a collector of more than 125,000 animal specimens. He married Annie Mitten (1848–1914), with whom he raised three children (Herbert died at age 4; Violet and William survived their father), published a highly successful narrative of his journey, *The Malay Archipelago: The Land of the Orang-Utan, and the Bird of Paradise* (1869), and wrote *Contributions to the Theory of Natural Selection* (1870). In the latter volume and in several articles from this period on human evolution and spiritualism, Wallace parted from the scientific naturalism of many of his friends and colleagues in claiming that natural selection could not account for the higher faculties of human beings.

The Wallace family moved several times, from Inner London to the outer borough of Barking, to Grays in Essex, and then south to Dorking, Surrey, to the outer borough of Croydon, to Godalming, Surrey, then to Parkstone and finally Broadstone, both in Dorset. Wallace built three of his family's houses, and at each he and his wife kept gardens. Although he applied for several jobs, Wallace never held a permanent position. He lost the profits from his collections through bad investments and other financial misfortunes. His income was limited to earnings from his writings, from grading school exams (which he did for some 25 years), and from a small inheritance from a relative. In 1881 he was added to the Civil List (i.e., granted a royal pension), thanks largely to the efforts of Darwin and Darwin's great advocate, the biologist and educator T.H. Huxley.

Wallace's two-volume *Geographical Distribution of Animals* (1876) and *Island Life* (1880) became the standard authorities in zoogeography and island biogeography, synthesizing knowledge about the distribution and dispersal of living and extinct animals in an evolutionary framework. For the ninth edition of Encyclopædia Britannica (1875–89), he wrote the article "Acclimatisation" (adaptation) and the animal life section of the article "Distribution." He also lectured in the British Isles and in the United States and traveled on the European continent. In addition to his major scientific works, Wallace actively pursued a variety of social and political interests. In writings and public appearances he opposed vaccination, eugenics, and vivisection while strongly supporting women's rights and land nationalization. Foremost among these commitments was an increasing engagement with spiritualism in his personal and public capacities.

Wallace received several awards, including the Royal Society of London's Royal Medal (1868), Darwin Medal (1890; for his independent origination of the origin of species by natural selection), Copley Medal (1908), and Order of Merit (1908); the Linnean Society of London's Gold Medal (1892) and Darwin-Wallace Medal (1908); and the Royal Geographical Society's Founder's Medal (1892). He was also awarded honorary doctorates from the Universities of Dublin (1882) and Oxford (1889) and won election to the Royal Society (1893).

Wallace published 21 books, and the list of his articles, essays, and letters in periodicals contains more than 700 items. Yet his career eludes simple description or honorifics. He was keenly intellectual but no less spiritual, a distinguished scientist and a spokesman for unpopular

causes, a gifted naturalist who never lost his boyish enthusiasm for nature, a prolific and lucid writer, a committed
socialist, a seeker of truth, and a domestic, modest individual. His engagement with progressive politics and
spiritualism likely contributed to his lack of employment
and to his somewhat peripheral status in the historical record. What touched those who knew him was his
compassion, his humanness and sympathy, and his lack of
pretense or acquired pride. Wallace died in his 91st year
and was buried in Broadstone, to be joined there by his
widow the following year. A commemorative medallion in
his honour was unveiled at Westminster Abbey in 1915.

HENRY WALTER BATES

(b. February 8, 1825, Leicester, Leicestershire,
England—d. February 16, 1892, London)

Henry Walter (H.W.) Bates was a British naturalist
and explorer whose demonstration of the operation
of natural selection in animal mimicry (the imitation by a
species of other life forms or inanimate objects), published
in 1861, gave firm support to Charles Darwin's theory of
evolution.

In 1844 Bates introduced the subject of entomology
to Alfred Russel Wallace, who in 1847 suggested a trip to
tropical jungles to collect specimens to sell at home and
to collect data that might help solve the problem of the
origin of species. On May 28, 1848, they arrived at Pará,
Brazil, near the mouth of the Amazon River. Wallace

H.W. Bates. Kean Collection/Archive Photos/Getty Images

returned to England in 1852; Bates remained 11 years, exploring the entire valley of the Amazon, where he collected about 14,712 species, mostly of insects, 8,000 previously unknown. On his return to England (1859), he began work on his huge collections and the preparation of his famous paper, presented in 1861 as "Contributions to an Insect Fauna of the Amazon Valley." In 1864 Bates was appointed assistant secretary of the Royal Geographical Society (London) and held the position until his death. He wrote *The Naturalist on the River Amazons*, 2 vol. (1863), and many papers on entomology.

JAMES AUGUSTUS GRANT

(b. April 11, 1827, Nairn, Nairn, Scotland—
d. February 11, 1892, Nairn)

The Scottish soldier and explorer James Augustus Grant accompanied John Hanning Speke in the search for and discovery of the source of the Nile River.

Commissioned in the British army in 1846, Grant saw action in India in the Sikh Wars and the Indian Mutiny of 1857–58. When Speke started his second African expedition in 1860, he asked Grant, his friend and comrade in India, to join him. A loyal lieutenant, Grant for long intervals during the expedition was given independent command of part of the caravan. After great hardship, they found the outlet of Lake Victoria from which the Nile issued (July 1862). For his services, Grant was awarded a gold medal by the Royal Geographical Society. During the 2 ½-year journey, Grant had kept a journal describing events of geographic significance and the customs of native peoples; it was published under the title *A Walk Across Africa* (1864). In 1868 Grant served in the intelligence department under Lord Napier during the Ethiopian campaign, retiring from the service that same year with the rank of lieutenant colonel.

JOHN HANNING SPEKE

(b. May 3, 1827, Bideford, Devon, England—
d. September 15, 1864, near Corsham, Wiltshire)

The British explorer John Hanning Speke was the first European to reach Lake Victoria in East Africa, which he correctly identified as a source of the Nile River. Commissioned in the British Indian Army in 1844, he served in the Punjab and traveled in the Himalayas and Tibet. In April 1855, as a member of Richard Burton's party attempting to explore Somaliland, Speke was severely wounded in an attack by the Somalis that broke up the expedition. In December 1856 he rejoined Burton on the island of Zanzibar. Their intention was to find a great lake said to lie in the heart of Africa and to be the origin of the Nile. After exploring the East African coast for six months to find the best route inland, the two men became the first Europeans to reach Lake Tanganyika (February 1858). During the return trip, Speke left Burton and struck out northward alone. On July 30 he reached the great lake, which he named in honour of Queen Victoria.

Speke's conclusion about the lake as a Nile source was rejected by Burton and was disputed by many in England, but the Royal Geographical Society, which had sponsored the expedition, honoured Speke for his exploits. On a second expedition (1860), he and James Grant mapped a portion of Lake Victoria. On July 28, 1862, Speke, not accompanied by Grant for this portion of the journey, found the Nile's exit from the lake and named it Ripon Falls. The party then tried to follow the river's course, but an outbreak of tribal warfare required them to change their route. In February 1863 they reached Gondokoro in the southern Sudan, where they met the Nile explorers Samuel Baker and Florence von Sass (who later became Baker's wife). Speke and Grant told them of another lake said to lie west of Lake Victoria. This information helped the Baker party to locate another Nile source, Lake Albert.

Speke's claim to have found the Nile source was again challenged in England, and, on the day he was to debate the subject publicly with Richard Burton, he was killed by his own gun while hunting. Accounts of his explorations were published in 1863 and 1864.

ADOLF ERIK, BARON NORDENSKIÖLD

(b. November 18, 1832, Helsinki, Finland—
d. August 12, 1901, Dalbyö, Sweden)

The Swedish geologist, mineralogist, geographer, and explorer Nils Adolf Erik, Baron (Frihere) Nordenskiöld sailed from Norway to the Pacific Ocean across the Asiatic Arctic, completing the first successful navigation of the Northeast Passage.

In 1858 Nordenskiöld settled in Stockholm, joined an expedition to the Arctic island of Spitsbergen, between Norway and Greenland, and became professor and curator of mineralogy at the Swedish State Museum. He returned to Spitsbergen again in 1861 and led his own expeditions there in 1864, 1868, and 1872–73, adding to geologic knowledge of the area. In 1870 he also led an expedition to western Greenland to study the inland ice.

Before attempting to cross the Northeast Passage, Nordenskiöld made preliminary voyages in 1875 and 1876, on which he penetrated the Kara Sea, north of Siberia, to the mouth of the Yenisey River. Sailing from Tromsø, Norway, aboard the steam vessel *Vega* on July 21, 1878, he reached Cape Chelyushkin, Siberia, roughly the midpoint of his journey, on August 19. From the end of September until July 18, 1879, the ship was frozen in near the Bering Strait. Resuming its course, the *Vega* reached Port Clarence, Alaska, on July 22 and returned to Europe by way of Guangzhou (now Canton, China), Ceylon (now Sri Lanka), and the Suez Canal. When Nordenskiöld reached Stockholm on April 24, 1880, he was made a baron by King Oscar. In 1883, while returning from western Greenland, where he penetrated far into the inland ice, he became the first to break through the great sea ice barrier of the southeast Greenland coast.

Nordenskiöld also made notable contributions in the field of cartography.

CHARLES GEORGE GORDON

(b. January 28, 1833, Woolwich, near London,
England—d. January 26, 1885, Khartoum, Sudan)

The British general Charles George ("Chinese") Gordon became a national hero for his exploits in China and for his ill-fated defense of Khartoum against the Mahdists.

Gordon, the son of an artillery officer, was commissioned a second lieutenant in the Royal Engineers in 1852. During the Crimean War (1853–56) he distinguished himself by his reckless bravery in the siege trenches outside Sevastopol. He was promoted to captain in 1859 and volunteered the following year to join the British forces that were fighting the Chinese in the second Opium War (1856–60) between the British and Chinese. He was present at the occupation of Beijing (October 1860) and personally directed the burning of the Chinese emperor's summer palace. In May 1862 Gordon's corps of engineers was assigned to strengthen the bulwarks of the European trading centre of Shanghai, which was being threatened by the insurgents of the Taiping Rebellion (1850–64). A year later he became commander of the 3,500-man peasant force, known as the "Ever-Victorious Army," raised to defend the city. During the next 18 months Gordon's troops played an important, though not a crucial, role in suppressing the Taiping uprising. He returned in January 1865 to England, where an enthusiastic public had already dubbed him "Chinese Gordon." For the next five years he was commander of the Royal Engineers at Gravesend, Kent; he spent his spare time developing his own unorthodox, mystical brand of Christianity and engaging in philanthropic activity among poor youths.

In 1873 the *khedive* (ruler) Ismāʻīl Pasha of Egypt, who regularly employed Europeans, appointed Gordon governor of the province of Equatoria in the Sudan. In Equatoria, from April 1874 to December 1876, Gordon mapped the upper Nile River and established a line of stations along the river as far south as present-day Uganda. After a brief stay in England, he resumed service under the khedive as governor-general of the Sudan. Gordon established his ascendancy over this vast area, crushing rebellions and suppressing the slave trade. Ill health forced him to resign and return to England in 1880; over the next two years he served in India, China, Mauritius, and Cape Colony (in southern Africa).

In 1884 Gordon was again sent to the Sudan by the British government to evacuate Egyptian forces from Khartoum, which was threatened by the Mahdists, followers of Muḥammad Aḥmad al-Mahdī. Reappointed governor-general, Gordon arrived in Khartoum in February. Khartoum came under siege a month later, and on January 26, 1885, the Mahdists broke into the city and killed Gordon and the other defenders. The British public reacted to his death by acclaiming "Gordon of Khartoum" a martyred warrior-saint and by blaming the government for failure to relieve the siege. However, some biographers, such as the noted Lytton Strachey, have suggested that Gordon, in defiance of his government's orders, had deliberately refused to evacuate Khartoum, even though evacuation was still possible until late in the siege.

NIKOLAY MIKHAYLOVICH PRZHEVALSKY

(b. March 31 [April 6, New Style], 1839, Smolensk, Russia—d. October 20 [November 1], 1888, Karakol, Russian Empire [now in Kyrgyzstan])

Nikolay Mikhaylovich Przhevalsky was a Russian traveler, who, by the extent of his explorations, route surveys, and plant and animal collections, added vastly to geographic knowledge of east-central Asia.

About 1869 Przhevalsky went to Irkutsk in central Siberia and in 1870 he set out from the region around Lake Baikal, traveled through to Urga (now Ulaanbaatar), Mongolia, and crossed the Gobi to reach China at Kalgan (Zhangjiakou) in Hebei province, 100 miles (160 km) from Beijing. His second journey began in 1876 at Kuldja (Yining) in the westernmost Xinjiang region of China and took him southeastward across the peaks of the Tien Shan and the drifting sands of the Takla Makan Desert to the foot of the

Nikolay Mikhaylovich Przhevalsky, monument in St. Petersburg. Sergey Kudryavtsev

Altun Mountains. His third journey brought him within 170 miles (270 km) of his goal, Lhasa, Tibet, but he was forbidden to enter the area. On his fourth and last trip, begun at Urga in 1883, he crossed the Gobi into Russian Turkistan and visited one of the largest mountain lakes in the world, Lake Ysyk (Ysyk-Köl). He died on the shores of the lake, at Karakol, which for a time was renamed Przhevalsk for him. His natural history discoveries include the wild camel and the wild horse, known as Przewalski's horse. His accounts of his first two journeys were both published in English translations: *Mongolia, the Tangut Country, and the Solitudes of Northern Tibet* (1876) and *From Kulja, Across the Tian Shan to Lop Nor* (1879).

SIR HENRY MORTON STANLEY

(b. January 28, 1841, Denbigh, Denbighshire,
Wales—d. May 10, 1904, London, England)

The British American explorer of central Africa Sir Henry Morton Stanley (born John Rowlands) became famous for his rescue of the Scottish missionary and explorer David Livingstone and for his discoveries in and development of the Congo region. He was knighted in 1899.

EARLY LIFE

Stanley's parents, John Rowlands and Elizabeth Parry, gave birth to him out of wedlock. He grew up partly in

the charge of reluctant relatives, partly in St. Asaph Workhouse. Modern research has shown his own account of ill treatment and a dramatic escape to be almost entirely a fantasy. There seem to have been no extraordinary events attending his departure from the workhouse at age 15, after receiving a reasonable education. The humiliations of institutional life and his mother's consistent neglect did, however, leave deep marks on his personality. After an interlude of dependence on relatives, he sailed from Liverpool as a cabin boy and landed at New Orleans in 1859.

There Rowlands was befriended by a merchant, Henry Hope Stanley, whose first and last names the boy adopted in an apparent effort to make a fresh start in life with a new identity; "Morton" was added later. Passages in Stanley's *Autobiography* concerning this period contain serious misstatements, particularly in regard to the movements of Mr. and Mrs. Henry Hope Stanley and the degree of intimacy that existed between them and young Rowlands. For some years Stanley led a roving life, as a soldier in the American Civil War, a seaman on merchant ships and in the U.S. Navy, and a journalist in the early days of frontier expansion; he even managed a trip to Turkey, recorded in *My Early Travels and Adventures in America and Asia* (1895).

In 1867 Stanley offered his services to James Gordon Bennett of the *New York Herald* as a special correspondent with the British expeditionary force sent against Tewodros II of Ethiopia, and Stanley was the first to report the fall of Magdala in 1868. An assignment to report on the Spanish Civil War followed, and in 1869 he received instructions to undertake a roving commission in the Middle East, which was to include the relief of Dr. David Livingstone, of whom little had been heard since his departure for Africa in 1866 to search for the source of the Nile River.

RELIEF OF LIVINGSTONE

On January 6, 1871, Stanley reached Zanzibar, the starting point for expeditions to the interior, and, intent on a scoop, left on March 21 without disclosing his intentions. His secretive conduct caused much offense to the authorities, especially to Sir John Kirk, the British consul, who had been having difficulty in making contact with Livingstone. Leading a well-equipped caravan and backed by American money, Stanley forced his way through country disturbed by fighting and stricken by sickness to Ujiji on Lake Tanganyika, Livingstone's last known port of call. There he found the old hero, ill and short of supplies, and greeted him with the famous words, "Dr. Livingstone, I presume?" (The exact date of their meeting is unclear, as both men recorded different dates in their journals; according to Stanley, they met on November 10, 1871, while Livingstone's journal suggests that the event occurred sometime between October 24 and 28.

A cordial friendship sprang up between the two men, and, when Stanley returned to the coast, he dispatched fresh supplies to enable Livingstone to carry on. The older man's quest ended a year later with his death in the swamps of Lake Bangweulu, still vainly seeking the Nile in a region that in fact gives rise to the Congo River.

How I Found Livingstone was published soon after Stanley's arrival in England in the late summer of 1872, when the exploits of this hitherto unknown adventurer gave rise to controversy. Members of the Royal Geographical Society (RGS) resented an American journalist having succeeded in relieving the famous traveler when they, his friends, had failed. Stanley did, however, receive the RGS Patron's Gold Medal. In 1873 Stanley went to Asante (Ashanti; now part of modern Ghana), again as a war correspondent for the *New York Herald* and in 1874 published his *Coomassie and Magdala: The Story of Two British Campaigns in Africa*.

DISCOVERY AND DEVELOPMENT OF THE CONGO

When Livingstone died in 1873, Stanley resolved to take up the exploration of Africa where he had left off. The problem of the Nile sources and the nature of the central African lakes had been only partly solved by earlier explorers. Stanley secured financial backing from the *New York Herald* and the *Daily Telegraph* of London for an expedition to pursue the quest, and the caravan left Zanzibar on November 12, 1874, heading for Lake Victoria. His visit to King Mutesa I of Buganda led to the admission of Christian missionaries to the area in 1877 and to the eventual establishment of a British protectorate in Uganda. Circumnavigating Lake Victoria, Stanley confirmed the explorer John H. Speke's estimate of its size and importance. Skirmishes with suspicious tribespeople on the lakeshore, which resulted in a number of casualties, gave rise in England to criticism of this new kind of traveler with his journalist's outlook and forceful methods. Lake Tanganyika was next explored and found to have no connection with the Nile system. Stanley and his men pressed on west to the Lualaba River (the very river that Livingstone had hoped was the Nile but that proved to be the headstream of the Congo). There they joined forces with the Arab trader Tippu Tib, who accompanied them for a few laps downriver, then left Stanley to fight his way first to Stanley Pool (now Malebo Pool) and then (partly overland) down to the great cataracts he named Livingstone Falls. Stanley and his men reached the sea on August 12, 1877, after an epic journey described in *Through the Dark Continent* (1878).

Failing to enlist British interests in the development of the Congo region, Stanley took service with the king of Belgium, Leopold II, whose secret ambition it was to annex the region for himself. From August 1879 to June 1884 Stanley was in the Congo basin, where he built a road from the lower Congo up to Stanley Pool and launched steamers on the upper river. (It is from this period, when Stanley persevered in the face of great difficulties, that he earned, from his men, the nickname of Bula Matari ["Breaker of Rocks"]). Originally under international auspices, Stanley's work was to pave the way for the creation of the Congo Free State, under the sovereignty of King

Leopold. These strenuous years are described in *The Congo and the Founding of Its Free State* (1885).

RELIEF OF EMIN PAŞA

Stanley's last expedition in Africa was for the relief of Mehmed Emin Paşa, governor of the Equatorial Province of Egypt, who had been cut off by the Mahdist revolt of 1882 in the environs of Lake Albert. Stanley was appointed to lead a relief expedition and decided to approach Lake Albert by way of the Congo River, counting on Tippu Tib to supply porters. Stanley left England in January 1887 and arrived at the mouth of the Congo in March. The expedition reached the navigable head of the river in June, and there, at Yambuya, Stanley left a rear column with orders to await Tippu Tib's porters. The failure of the rear column to rejoin the main body later gave rise to controversy harmful to Stanley's reputation. Eventually the expedition was assembled at Lake Albert, and, despite Emin's initial reluctance to leave his province, an entourage of some 1,500 people set out for the east coast on April 10, 1889, and arrived at Bagamoyo on December 4. On the way, the Ruwenzori Range was revealed to explorers for the first time (identified as Ptolemy's Mountains of the Moon), and the Semliki River was shown to link Lakes Edward and Albert; thus were cleared up the few doubtful geographic points regarding the Nile sources. *In Darkest Africa* (1890) is Stanley's own account of his last adventure on the African continent. He received a Special Gold Medal from the RGS.

Stanley married Dorothy Tennant on July 12, 1890, and they adopted a son, Denzil. Stanley was renaturalized a British subject in 1892 (he had become a U.S. citizen on

May 15, 1885) and sat in Parliament as Liberal Unionist for North Lambeth from 1895 to 1900. In 1897 he visited South Africa and wrote *Through South Africa* (1898). He was made a Knight Grand Cross of the Order of the Bath in 1899, becoming Sir Henry Morton Stanley. The remaining years before his death were spent mainly at Furze Hill near Pirbright, Surrey, a small estate that he bought in 1898.

GEORGE WALLACE MELVILLE

(b. July 31, 1841, New York, New York, U.S.—
d. March 17, 1912, Philadelphia)

The American Arctic explorer and naval engineer George Wallace Melville led the sole surviving party from George Washington De Long's tragic expedition attempting to reach the North Pole.

Melville entered the U.S. Navy in 1861 and in 1879 joined De Long's crew on the *Jeanette*. When the vessel became lodged in the ice off northeastern Siberia, Melville's engineering skill helped keep it afloat for almost two years until it was finally crushed. After a long, arduous journey by boat and sledge, Melville and a group of men reached the Siberian shore and obtained help at the mouth of the Lena River. He then led an expedition that found the remains of De Long and his party the following spring. The incredible hardships the searchers endured on their 500-mile (800-km) trek are modestly told in Melville's *In the Lena*

Delta (1884). He was again chief engineer aboard the *Thetis* on a mission that in June 1884 rescued the survivors from Adolphus Washington Greely's Arctic expedition.

In 1887 Melville became engineer in chief of the U.S. Navy. During a period when a modern navy was being built, he designed machinery for 120 ships of more than 700,000 horsepower. For a decade, two of them were the fastest warships afloat. He introduced various engineering improvements, including the triple screw (a propeller system) and the vertical boiler. Before his retirement as rear admiral in 1903, he brought about a general reform of the naval engineering department.

CHARLES MONTAGU DOUGHTY

(b. August 19, 1843, Theberton Hall, Leiston,
Suffolk, England—d. January 20, 1926,
Sissinghurst, Kent)

The British adventurer Charles Montagu Doughty is widely regarded as one of the greatest of all Western travelers in Arabia.

After attending London and Cambridge universities, he traveled widely in Europe, Egypt, the Holy Land, and Syria. He began his journey to northwestern Arabia at Damascus in 1876 and proceeded southward with pilgrims headed for Mecca as far as Madā'in Ṣāliḥ. There he studied monuments and inscriptions left by the ancient Nabataean civilization. His observations were published by Ernest Renan. On the latter part of his journey, however, which included visits to Taymāʾ, Ḥāʾil, ʿUnayzah, at-Ṭāʾif, and Jidda, he made his most important geographical, geological, and anthropological observations.

In 1888 he published *Travels in Arabia Deserta*, which won little recognition at the time, though it eventually came to be regarded as a masterpiece of travel writing. In it he was more concerned with producing a monument of what he considered to be pure English prose than with recording information. The Elizabethan style in which it is cast succeeds in conveying the feeling of his remote and lonely wandering. Doughty himself, however, attached more importance to his epic and dramatic poetry. These works include *The Dawn in Britain*, 6 vol. (1906), *The Clouds* (1912), and *Mansoul* (1920).

VERNEY LOVETT CAMERON

(b. July 1, 1844, Radipole, near Weymouth, Dorset, England—d. March 27, 1894, near Leighton Buzzard, Bedfordshire)

The British explorer Verney Lovett Cameron was the first European to cross equatorial Africa from sea to sea.

Cameron entered the British navy in 1857, taking part in the Abyssinian campaign of 1868 and in the suppression of the East African slave trade. In 1872 the Royal Geographical Society chose him to lead an expedition to take help to the explorer David Livingstone, who was presumed lost in eastern Africa, and also to explore on his own. Soon after leaving Zanzibar, the expedition met Livingstone's servants bearing his body. At Ujiji on Lake Tanganyika, Cameron recovered some of Livingstone's papers. Exploring the southern half of the lake, he established its outlet at the Lukuga River, a Congo tributary. He then traced the Congo-Zambezi watershed for hundreds of miles and reached the west coast of Africa near Benguela, Angola, on November 7, 1875.

He wrote *Across Africa* (1877) and for the rest of his life was associated with developing commercial projects in Africa. Claiming to have originated the idea of a "Cape to Cairo" railway, which English-born South African financier and statesman Cecil Rhodes endeavoured to develop, Cameron also advocated an African-Asian railway from Tripoli, Libya, to Karachi (now in Pakistan). He visited western Africa with Sir Richard Burton, with whom he wrote *To the Gold Coast for Gold* (1883).

GEORGE WASHINGTON DE LONG

(b. August 22, 1844, New York, New York,
U.S.—d. October 30, 1881, Siberia [Russia])

George Washington De Long was the American explorer who led the disastrous Arctic expedition that gave evidence of a continuous ocean current across the polar regions.

De Long conceived of a plan for reaching the North Pole while serving with a polar expedition that sailed around Greenland in 1873. Setting sail from San Francisco in July 1879, he took the *Jeannette* through the Bering Strait and headed for Wrangel Island, off the northeast coast of Siberia. At the time, many believed that Wrangel was a large landmass stretching far to the north, and De Long hoped to sail as far as possible along its coast and then to sled to the Pole. On September 5, however, the ship became trapped in the pack ice near Herald Island (now Gerald Island), east of Wrangel. While drifting north-westward for 21 months, De Long discovered the limited extent of Wrangel.

At 77°15' N, 155° E, northeast of the New Siberian Islands, the *Jeannette* was crushed by ice (June 12, 1881) and sank the following day. The crew, including De Long, escaped with most of their provisions and three small boats. Their destination, the Siberian coast, lay some 600 miles (1,000 km) away. They endured extreme hardships for the next two months as they crossed the ice. After reaching open water, one of the boats and the men aboard were lost. The remaining boats became separated; De Long's reached the eastern side of the Lena River delta, and his engineer, George Melville, reached the western side. Melville's party was rescued, but De Long and his men died of exposure and starvation.

De Long's journal, in which he made regular entries until shortly before his death, was found a year later and published as *The Voyage of the* Jeannette (1883). Three years after the *Jeannette* was sunk, wreckage from it was found on an ice floe on the southwest coast of Greenland, a discovery that gave new support to the theory of trans-Arctic drift.

ALEKSANDR MIKHAYLOVICH SIBIRYAKOV

(b. September 26 [October 8, New Style], 1849,
Irkutsk, Siberia, Russian Empire—d. 1893)

Aleksandr Mikhaylovich Sibiryakov (or Sibiriakov) was a Russian gold-mine proprietor who was noted for both his financing of explorations in Siberia and for his own expeditions in the area.

Sibiryakov was a graduate of a polytechnic school in Zürich, Switzerland. A wealthy man, he financed the scientific expeditions of the Swedish explorer Adolf Erik Nordenskiöld (1878–79) and the Russian explorer A.V. Grigoryev (1879–80) into the polar regions and facilitated the publication of works on Siberian history. In 1880 he made his first exploratory expedition—on the Kara Sea. In 1884, in his most famous trek, he sailed in a steamer to the mouth of the Pechora River, traveled by reindeer eastward to and across the Ural Mountains, and followed the Tobol River to Tobolsk, the traditional stepping-off point to Siberia. This route, later much traveled, became known as Sibiryakov's Route to the North.

An island in the Kara Sea is named for him. A famous icebreaker, built in 1909 in Glasgow and named the *Sibiryakov* after purchase by Russia in 1916, was used in both World Wars (being sunk by a German cruiser in 1942) and was the first ship to make a nonstop voyage across the North from the White Sea to the Bering Sea (1932).

EDUARD ROBERT FLEGEL

(b. October 13, 1855, Vilna, Lithuania, Russian
Empire—d. September 11, 1886, Brass, Nigeria)

The German explorer of Africa Eduard Robert Flegel
was the first European to reach the source of the
Benue River.

In 1879 Flegel traveled about 525 miles (845 km) up
the Benue River and in 1880 went by way of the Niger to
Sokoto, in northwestern Nigeria, where he obtained permission from the sultan there for an expedition to the
Adamawa Plateau. In the course of exploring the Benue
River basin (1882–84), he reached the Benue's source,
near Ngaoundéré, now in Cameroon. After a short stay
in Europe, Flegel returned to Africa in April 1885 with a
commission to open up the Niger and Benue basins to
German commercial influence and thus prevent British
ascendancy in that region. He was, however, unsuccessful
and died the following year. His works include *Lose Blätter
aus dem Tagebuch meiner Haussa-Freunde und Reisegefährten*
(1885; "Loose Leaves from the Diary of My Hausa Friends
and Travel Companions") and *Vom Niger-Benüe* (1890;
"Concerning the Niger-Benue").

FRIDTJOF NANSEN

(b. October 10, 1861, Store-Frøen, near Kristiania [now Oslo], Norway— d. May 13, 1930, Lysaker, near Oslo)

Norwegian explorer, oceanographer, statesman, and humanitarian Fridtjof Nansen led a number of expeditions to the Arctic (1888, 1893, 1895–96) and oceanographic expeditions in the North Atlantic Ocean (1900, 1910–14). For his relief work after World War I he was awarded the Nobel Prize for Peace (1922).

Fridtjof Nansen, 1896. Hulton Archive/Getty Images

EARLY LIFE

Nansen went to school in Kristiania (Oslo), where in 1880 he passed his entrance examination to the university. He chose to study zoology in the expectation that fieldwork would give him the chance of an outdoor life and enable him to make use of his artistic talents. Although scientific work was always closest to his heart, he first attained fame as an explorer.

As a young man Nansen was a great outdoor athlete, an accomplished skater and skier, and a keen hunter and fisherman. In 1882, when he joined the sealing ship *Viking* for a voyage to the Greenland waters, Nansen first saw at a distance Greenland's mighty ice cap. It occurred to him that it ought to be possible to cross it, and gradually he developed a plan, which he announced in 1887. Instead of starting from the inhabited west coast, he would start from the east coast and, by cutting off his means of retreat,

Hand-coloured lantern slide of Fridtjof Nansen's North Pole expedition, c. 1895. Imagno/Hulton Archive/Getty Images

would force himself to go forward. The expedition of six from Norway started the crossing on August 15, 1888. After enduring storms and intense cold, they reached the highest point of the journey (8,920 feet [2,719 metres]) on September 5 and struck the west coast at Ameralik fjord on September 26. They were forced to winter at the settlement of Godthåb (Nuuk), where Nansen took the opportunity to study the Inuit (Eskimos) and gather material for his book *Eskimoliv* (1891; Eskimo Life). The party returned home in triumph in May 1889.

In 1890 Nansen presented before the Norwegian Geographical Society a plan for an even more hazardous expedition. Having collected evidence showing that the ice of the polar sea drifted from Siberia toward Spitsbergen, he proposed to build a ship of such a shape that it would be lifted but not crushed when caught by the ice. He proposed to let this ship freeze in off eastern Siberia in order to be carried from there across the Arctic Ocean to Spitsbergen by the currents. Though his plan was severely criticized by contemporary Arctic explorers, the Norwegian Parliament granted two-thirds of the estimated expenses, and the rest was raised by subscriptions from King Oscar II and private individuals. His ship, *Fram* ("Forward"; now preserved outside Oslo), was built according to his ideas.

With a complement of 13 men, the *Fram* sailed from Kristiania on June 24, 1893. On September 22 it was enclosed by the ice at 78°50' N, 133°37' E; it froze in, and the long drift began. It bore the pressure of the ice perfectly. On March 14, 1895, Nansen, being satisfied that the *Fram* would continue to drift safely, left it in 84°4' N, 102°27' E, and started northward with dogsleds and kayaks, accompanied by F.H. Johansen. On April 8 they turned back from 86°14' N, the highest latitude then yet reached by humans, and headed toward Franz Josef Land. As they approached the northern islands, progress was hampered by open water and, because of the advanced season, they wintered on Frederick Jackson Island (named by Nansen for the British Arctic explorer), where they stayed from August 26, 1895, to May 19, 1896. They built a hut of stone and covered it with a roof of walrus hides and lived during the winter mainly on polar bear and walrus meat, using the blubber as fuel. On their way to Spitsbergen they encountered Frederick Jackson and his party of the Jackson-Harmsworth expedition, on June 17, and returned to Norway in his ship *Windward*, reaching Vardø on August 13. The *Fram* also reached Norway safely, having drifted north to 85°57'. Nansen and his companions on board the *Fram* were given a rousing welcome, which reached its climax on their arrival in Kristiania on September 9. His two-volume account of the expedition, *Fram over Polhavet* (*Farthest North*), appeared in 1897.

SCIENTIFIC WORK

Nansen's success as an explorer was due largely to his careful evaluation of the difficulties that might be encountered, his clear reasoning, which was never influenced by the opinions of others, his willingness to accept a calculated risk, his thorough planning, and his meticulous attention to detail. Many of these traits can be recognized in his scientific writings. In 1882 he was appointed curator of zoology at the Bergen museum. He wrote papers on zoological and histological subjects, illustrated by excellent drawings. For one of his papers, "The Structure and Combination of Histological Elements of the Central Nervous System" (1887), the University of Kristiania conferred upon him the degree of doctor of philosophy. Though the paper contained so many novel interpretations that the committee that had to examine it accepted it with doubt, it is now considered a classic.

On his return from the *Fram* expedition in 1896, a professorship in zoology was established for Nansen at the University of Kristiania, but his interests shifted from zoology to physical oceanography, and in 1908 his status was changed to professor of oceanography. During 1896–1917 he devoted most of his time and energy to scientific work. He edited the report of the scientific results of his expedition and himself wrote some of the most important parts. He participated in the establishment of the International Council for the Exploration of the Sea and for some time directed the council's central laboratory in Kristiania. In 1900 he joined the *Michael Sars* on a cruise in the Norwegian Sea. In 1910 he made a cruise in the *Fridtjof* through the northeastern North Atlantic; in 1912 he visited the Spitsbergen waters on board his own yacht *Veslemoy*; and in 1914 he joined B. Helland-Hansen on an oceanographic cruise to the Azores in the *Armauer Hansen*. In 1913 Nansen traveled through the Barents Sea and the Kara Sea to the mouth of the Yenisey River and back through Siberia. He published the results of his cruises in numerous papers, partly in cooperation with Helland-Hansen. His lasting contributions to oceanography comprise improvement and design of instruments, explanation of the wind-driven currents of the seas, discussions of the waters of the Arctic, and explanation of the manner in which deep- and bottom-water is formed.

Nansen also dealt with other subjects: for instance, his *Nord i tåkeheimen*, 2 vol. (1911; *In Northern Mists*) gave a critical review of the exploration of the northern regions from early times up to the beginning of the 16th century.

STATESMAN AND HUMANITARIAN

As Nansen grew older he became more interested in the relations between individuals and countries. In 1905 he took a lively part in the discussion about the dissolution of the union between Norway and Sweden. His attitude may be summarized by his words: "Any union in which the one people is restrained in exercising its freedom is and will remain a danger." On the establishment of the Norwegian monarchy, Nansen was appointed its first minister in London (1906–08). In 1917, during World War I, he was appointed head of a Norwegian commission to the United States and negotiated a satisfactory agreement with the U.S. government about the import of essential supplies to Norway.

At the first assembly of the League of Nations in 1920, the Norwegian delegation was headed by Nansen, who was to remain one of the outstanding members of the assembly until his death. In April 1920 the council of the League of Nations gave Nansen his first great task, appointing him high commissioner responsible for the repatriation from Russia of about 500,000 prisoners of war from the former German and Austro-Hungarian armies. The Soviet government would not recognize the League of Nations but negotiated with Nansen personally, and in September 1922 he reported to the third assembly of the League that his task was completed and that 427,886 prisoners of war had been repatriated.

In August 1921 Nansen was asked by the International Committee of the Red Cross to direct an effort to bring relief to famine-stricken Russia. He accepted, and on August

15 a conference in Geneva, at which 13 governments and 48 Red Cross organizations were represented, appointed him high commissioner of this new venture. On August 27 he concluded an agreement with the Soviet government authorizing him to open in Moscow an office of the "International Russian Relief Executive." Nansen's request to the League for financial assistance was turned down, but by appealing to private organizations and by addressing large public meetings he succeeded in raising the necessary funds.

On July 5, 1922, on Nansen's initiative, an international agreement was signed in Geneva introducing the identification card for displaced persons known as the "Nansen passport." In 1931 the Nansen International Office for Refugees was created in Geneva (after Nansen's death); it cared mainly for anticommunist ("White") Russians, for Armenians from Turkey, and, later, for Jews from Nazi Germany.

In 1922 Nansen was awarded the Nobel Prize for Peace; he used the prize money for the furtherance of international relief work. The Nansen International Office for Refugees won the Nobel Prize for Peace in 1938.

MARY HENRIETTA KINGSLEY

(b. November 13, 1862, London, England—
d. June 3, 1900, Simonstown, near Cape Town,
Cape Colony [now in South Africa])

Mary Henrietta Kingsley was an English traveler who, disregarding the conventions of her time, journeyed through western and equatorial Africa and became the first European to enter parts of Gabon.

A niece of the clergyman and author Charles Kingsley, she led a secluded life until she was about 30, when she decided to go to West Africa to study African religion and law, with a view to completing a book left unfinished by her deceased father, George Henry Kingsley. During 1893 and 1894 she visited Cabinda, the coastal enclave of Angola lying today between Congo (Kinshasa) and Congo (Brazzaville); Old Calabar in southeast Nigeria; and the island of Fernando Po, now Bioko in Equatorial Guinea, near the Cameroon coast. Around the lower Congo River she collected specimens of beetles and freshwater fishes for the British Museum. Returning to Africa in December 1894, she visited the French Congo and, in Gabon, ascended the Ogooué River through the country of the Fang, a tribe with a reputation for cannibalism. On this journey she had many harrowing adventures and narrow escapes. She then visited Corisco Island, off Gabon, and also climbed Mount Cameroon.

THE LATE MISS KINGSLEY

Mary Henrietta Kingsley. Illustrated London News/Hulton Archvie/Getty Images

After returning to England with valuable natural history collections, she lectured widely throughout the country about her travels (1896–99). Her writings, which express her strong sympathies for black Africans, include *Travels in West Africa* (1897) and *West African Studies* (1899). She died while nursing sick prisoners during the South African (Boer) War.

SIR FRANCIS EDWARD YOUNGHUSBAND

(b. May 31, 1863, Murree, India—d. July 31, 1942, Lytchett Minster, Dorset, England)

Sir Francis Edward Younghusband was a British army officer and explorer whose travels, mainly in northern India and Tibet, yielded major contributions to geographical research. He also forced the conclusion of the Anglo-Tibetan Treaty (September 6, 1904) that gained Britain long-sought trade concessions.

Younghusband entered the army in 1882 and in 1886–87 crossed Central Asia from Beijing to Yarkand (now in the Uygur Autonomous Region of Xinjiang, China). Continuing on to India by way of the long-unused Mustagh (Muztag) Pass of the Karakoram Range, he proved the range to be the water divide between India and Turkistan. On two later expeditions to Central Asia he explored the Pamirs (mountain system).

After repeated British attempts to gain trading rights with Tibet, Lord Curzon, viceroy of India, authorized

Younghusband to cross the Tibetan border accompanied by a military escort to negotiate trade and frontier issues (July 1903). When efforts to begin negotiations failed, the British, under the command of Major General James Macdonald, invaded the country and slaughtered some 600 Tibetans at Guru. Younghusband moved on to Jiangzi (Gyantze), where his second attempt to begin trade negotiations also failed. He then marched into Lhasa, the capital, with British troops and forced the conclusion of a trade treaty with the Dalai Lama, Tibet's ruler. This action brought him a knighthood in 1904.

ADRIEN-VICTOR-JOSEPH, BARON DE GERLACHE DE GOMERY

(b. August 2, 1866, Hasselt, Belgium—
d. December 4, 1934, Brussels)

The Belgian naval officer Adrien-Victor-Joseph, baron de Gerlache de Gomery led the first Antarctic expedition concentrating on scientific observation (1897–99). Sailing with him as mate on the *Belgica* was Roald Amundsen, who on a subsequent expedition of his own was the first to reach the South Pole. After making discoveries north of Graham (Palmer) Land, de Gerlache navigated the *Belgica* into the pack ice, where it remained trapped for 13 months and thus became the first vessel to winter in the Antarctic.

De Gerlache sailed to the Persian Gulf to collect zoological specimens (1901). He also conducted oceanographic studies—off the east coast of Greenland (1905), north of Scandinavia and Russia in the Barents and Kara seas (1907), and in the Barents and Greenland seas (1909). He made an overland crossing of Greenland from west to east at $77°$ N in 1909. De Gerlache assisted the English explorer Sir Ernest Shackleton in planning the British Imperial Trans-Antarctic Expedition of 1914 to 1917.

CONCLUSION

The explorers and adventurers of the 19th century largely completed the quests started by their predecessors more than a half millennium earlier. By the end of the century continental coastlines had been fully defined, and the interiors of these landmasses had been penetrated, studied, and described to a fascinated and eager public. The corners of Earth that were not yet known had largely been reduced to the most remote and inaccessible places—the two poles, the highest mountains, and the depths of the oceans being especially notable among them—as those goals awaited the advances in expertise and technology that would make attaining them possible in the next century. The world was a much smaller place in 1900 than it had been in 1800, thanks in large part to dramatic advances in transportation and communication and to the vanguard work of the explorers and adventurers who everywhere pushed back the veils of geographic ignorance.

Those intrepid men—and they were nearly all men and Europeans or North Americans of European ancestry—were at the forefront of the dawn of the modern age. In North America, in the first decade of the century, Meriwether Lewis and William Clark undertook their remarkable three-year journey through the heart of western North America, thus revealing to the still-young United States that region's vastness and richness. Explorers of the African interior such as David Livingstone, Sir Richard Burton, John Speke, and Sir Henry Morton Stanley filled in much of the map on the so-called "dark" continent and paved the way for Europe's rapid colonization there in the 19th and early 20th centuries. Such was also the case in Australia, where information on the continent's huge dry interior gained from explorers such as John Oxley, Charles Sturt, Ludwig Leichhardt, and Sir Thomas Livingstone Mitchell allowed other Europeans to penetrate inland from the colonies on the coastal fringes.

The feats and importance of those men, however, must be put in perspective with the contributions of many others in the 19th century whose accomplishments did so much to advance scientific and cultural knowledge at the time. To be sure, considerable scientific information was gained by Lewis and Clark and by other journeys of exploration. Beginning with Alexander von Humboldt—whose sojourn in South America was contemporaneous with the Lewis and Clark odyssey—and others such as Charles Darwin and Alfred Russel Wallace after him, however, the primary focus was on collecting, studying, and classifying the myriad wonders of life on Earth. Their efforts not only vastly enriched human understanding of the natural world but were instrumental in refining the precepts of the scientific method that had come out of the Enlightenment. Whole new branches of natural science emerged, notably that based on Darwin's theory of evolution, and many others advanced significantly, such as oceanography through the work of Fridtjof Nansen in the Arctic. In the social sciences, archaeologist Heinrich Schliemann and his successor, Wilhelm Dörpfeld, demonstrated the existence of a previously unknown ancient Greek civilization through their discovery and excavation of Troy and other archaeological sites.

Thus, the world in 1900 was not only a much smaller but also a vastly different place than it had been a century earlier. Explorers and adventurers had made possible or accelerated the rate of change by their often audacious feats and undertakings. By 1900, however, the challenges left were so great that they usually required more of the studied and calculated approach of a Nansen than the derring-do and brashness of a Burton if they were to be conquered. Finally, for as extraordinary as were the accomplishments of those truly remarkable people during the 19th century, they would pale in comparison to what was to come in the succeeding decades.

GLOSSARY

ad hoc Created for the particular end or case at hand without consideration of wider application.

agnostic One who is not committed to believing in either the existence or the nonexistence of God or a god.

aide-de-camp One who acts as an assistant; for example, a military officer who acts as an assistant to a superior officer.

alcalde A traditional community-elected leader.

angina Disease marked by spasmodic attacks of intense suffocative pain.

barrow Large mound of earth or stones over the remains of the dead.

Bear Flag Revolt (June–July 1846) Short-lived independence rebellion precipitated by American settlers in California's Sacramento Valley against Mexican authorities.

biogeography Study of the geographic distribution of plants and animals.

brig Two-masted sailing ship with square rigging on both masts.

cacao bean Dried, partly fermented fatty seeds of a South American evergreen tree that are used in making cocoa, chocolate, and cocoa butter.

Calvinist Theological system of French theologian and reformer John Calvin and his followers marked by strong emphasis on the sovereignty of God, the depravity of humanity, and the doctrine of predestination.

cant Language that is hypocritically pious and moralizing.

cartographer One who makes maps.

cataract Waterfall (especially a large one over a precipice).

chargé d'affaires Low-ranking diplomatic representative.

consort Spouse of a reigning monarch.

consul Official appointed by a government to reside in a foreign country to represent the commercial interests of citizens of the appointing country.

corpus All the writings or works of a particular kind or on a particular subject.

crampons Sets of sharp spikes that can be strapped onto the boots to provide surer footing on ice.

declaim Deliver an oration in a theatrical manner.

delta Triangular or fan-shaped piece of land made by deposits of mud and sand at the mouth of a river.

Dissenter (Also called Nonconformist or Free Churchman), any English Protestant who does not conform to the doctrines or practices of the established Church of England.

doyen One uniquely skilled by long experience in some field of endeavour.

dysentery Disease characterized by severe diarrhea with passage of mucus and blood from the bowels.

emigrate To leave a country or region to live elsewhere.

ensign Naval commissioned officer of the lowest rank.

entomology Branch of zoology that focuses on the study of insects.

eugenics The often-controversial science that attempts to select desirable heritable characteristics in order to improve future generations; typically applied to humans.

fauna Animals or animal life especially of a region, period, or environment.

flora Plants or plant life especially of a region, period, or environment.

frigate Medium-sized square-rigged warship.

gaucho Cowboy of the South American grass-covered plains (Pampas).

genera Plural form of genus (genus being a class, kind, or group marked by common characteristics or by one common characteristic).

herbarium Collection of dried plant specimens.

hermaphrodite Animal or plant having both male and female reproductive organs.

hydrography The art and science of compiling and producing charts, or maps, of water-covered areas of the Earth's surface.

impecunious Having very little or no money (usually habitually).

indigo Valuable blue vat dye obtained from plants (as indigo plants).

keelboat Small riverboat.

magistrate Official with some judicial power.

magnetometer Instrument used to detect the presence of a metallic object or to measure the strength of a magnetic field.

medium One through whom others seek to communicate with the spirits of the dead.

mesmerism Hypnotism.

ordinand One about to be ordained.

pangenesis Disproven hypothetical mechanism of heredity in which the cells throw off particles that collect in the reproductive products or in buds so that the egg or bud contains particles from all parts of the parent.

parish In some Christian church groups, a geographic unit served by a pastor or priest. It is a subdivision of a diocese (the territorial jurisdiction of a bishop).

parsonage The house provided by a church for its pastor.

paymaster Officer or agent of a government, a corporation, or an employer whose duty it is to pay salaries or wages and keep account of them.

philologist One who loves learning or literature; a scholar especially of classical antiquity.

phrenology Pseudoscientific system based on the idea that indentations and convolutions form on the human skull because of the presence or absence of certain mental faculties.

pirogue Canoe-like boat.

plenipotentiary Invested with full power.

polymath One possessing encyclopedic learning.

portage Route for the carrying of boats or goods overland from one body of water to another.

Punjab Region in eastern Pakistan and northwestern India in valley of the Indus River.

rhea Either of two large three-toed South American birds that cannot fly and resemble (but are smaller than) the African ostrich.

rookery Place where a group of birds or social mammals (as penguins or seals) breed, nest, or raise their young.

schooner Ship with a fore-and-aft rig and two or more masts.

séance Spiritualist meeting in which participants attempt to communicate with spirits.

sledge Strong, heavy sled.

straitened Impoverished.

stratigraphy Scientific discipline concerned with the description of rock successions and their interpretation in terms of a general time scale.

subaltern Junior officer.

taxonomy The study of the general principles of scientific classification.

uniformitarian One who advocates uniformitarianism, namely, a geological doctrine that explains geologic features as being the result of uniform forces at present and over long spans of time—from the origin of Earth to the present day.

viscera Internal organs, such as the liver and intestines. (Plural form of viscus.)

vivisection Any form of animal experimentation (such as a surgical operation) especially if considered to cause distress to a live subject.

wastrel Waster; good-for-nothing.

waterman Boatman who is skilled in the ways of watercraft.

zoogeography Branch of biogeography concerned with the geographic distribution of animals and especially with the determination of the areas characterized by specific groups of animals and the study of the causes and significance of such groups.

BIBLIOGRAPHY

Two informative overviews on the exploration of continental interiors are Margery Perham and J. Simmons (eds.), *African Discovery*, 2nd ed. (1957, reissued 1971); and Ernest Scott (ed.), *Australian Discovery*, 2 vol. (1929, reprinted 1966), with a wide selection of passages from the journals of explorers. Clements R. Markham, *The Lands of Silence: A History of Arctic and Antarctic Exploration* (1921, reprinted 2004), discusses the early decades of expeditions to the polar regions. Standard biographies of Humboldt include Helmut De Terra, *Humboldt: The Life and Times of Alexander von Humboldt, 1769–1859* (1955, reprinted 1979); L. (Charlotte) Kellner, *Alexander von Humboldt* (1963); and Douglas Botting, *Humboldt and the Cosmos* (1973, reissued 2007).

There is a rich literature on Lewis and Clark's monumental odyssey and its aftermath. Stephen D. Beckham (ed.), *The Literature of the Lewis and Clark Expedition: A Bibliography and Essays* (2003), chronicles 200 years of these publications. Gary E. Moulton (ed.), *The Journals of the Lewis and Clark Expedition*, 13 vol. (1979–2001), remains the definitive edition, with an atlas (vol. 1), herbarium (vol. 12), and index (vol. 13); there is also a one-volume version, *The Lewis and Clark Journals: An American Epic of Discovery* (2003). David Lavender, *The Way to the Western Sea: Lewis and Clark Across the Continent* (1988, reissued 2001), is an engaging narrative account. As for the participants themselves, biographies on the two leaders include William E. Foley, *Wilderness Journey: The Life of William Clark* (2004), the best treatment; Landon Y. Jones, *William Clark and the Shaping of the West* (2004), which examines how Clark both influenced and was affected by the forces of his day; Stephen E. Ambrose, *Undaunted Courage: Meriwether Lewis, Thomas Jefferson, and the Opening of the American West* (1996, reissued 2003), which focuses on Lewis's role in the expedition; and Richard H. Dillon, *Meriwether Lewis: A Biography* (1965, reissued 2003), a reliable account. Works on Sacagawea include Grace R. Hebard, *Sacajawea, a Guide and Interpreter of the Lewis and Clark Expedition* (1932, reissued 2002); and Harold P. Howard, *Sacajawea* (1971, reissued 2001), the best narrative biography.

Ernest S. Dodge, *The Polar Rosses* (1973); and M.J. Ross, *Polar Pioneers: John Ross and James Clark Ross* (1994), focus on John Ross and his nephew. Sir John Franklin's life and achievements are portrayed in Paul Nanton, *Arctic Breakthrough: Franklin's Expeditions, 1819–1847* (1970, reissued 1981); Leslie H. Neatby, *The Search for Franklin* (1970); and Roderic Owen, *The Fate of Franklin* (1978). Subsequent revisionist theories of the expedition's fate include Owen Beattie and John Geiger, *Frozen in Time* (1987, reissued 2004), detailing the forensic study of the exhumed bodies of three expedition sailors; and David C. Woodman, *Unravelling the Franklin Mystery: Inuit Testimony* (1991). Liv Nansen Høyer, *Nansen, a Family Portrait*, trans. from the Norwegian by Maurice Michael (1957), was written by Fridtjof Nansen's daughter. Roland Huntford, *Nansen: The Explorer as Hero* (1997, reissued 2001), is a comprehensive biography.

Biographies of Charles Darwin include Adrian Desmond and James Moore, *Darwin* (1992); Janet Browne, *Charles Darwin*, 2 vol. (1996–2002); and Peter J. Bowler, *Charles Darwin: The Man and His Influence* (1990, reissued and reprinted 2000), an overview of Darwin's century. Nora Barlow (ed.), *The Autobiography of Charles Darwin, 1809–1882, With Original Omissions Restored* (1958, reissued 1993 and 2010), is his unexpurgated autobiography. Standard sources on Darwin's friend and colleague Alfred Russel Wallace include his autobiography, *My Life: A Record of Events and Opinions*, 2 vol. (1905, reissued 1974); and James Marchant, *Alfred Russel Wallace: Letters and Reminiscences* (1916, reprinted 1975). Among biographies on him are Harry Clements, Alfred Russel Wallace (1983); Martin Fichman, Alfred Russel Wallace (1981); and the lavishly illustrated Timothy Severin, *The Spice Islands Voyage* (1997), a combined biography-travelogue that traces Wallace's work in the Malay Archipelago.

The fundamental works of David Livingstone are *Missionary Travels and Researches in South Africa* (1857, reprinted 1972), *Dr. Livingstone's Cambridge Lectures*, ed. by William Monk (1858, reprinted 1968), *Narrative of an Expedition to the Zambesi and Its Tributaries: And of the Discovery of the Lakes Shirwa and Nyassa: 1858–1864* (1865, reissued 2001), and *The Last Journals of David Livingstone in Central Africa, from 1865 to His Death*, 2 vol., ed. by Horace Waller (1874, reprinted 1970). Among the most useful biographies are Bridglal Pachai (ed.), *Livingstone: Man of Africa: Memorial Essays, 1873–1973* (1973); and George Seaver, *David Livingstone: His Life and Letters* (1957). More recent works include Rob Mackenzie, *David Livingstone: The Truth Behind the Legend*, 8th ed. (2005); and Andrew Ross, *David Livingstone: Mission and Empire* (2006).

Biographies of Sir Richard Burton by his contemporaries include Isabel Burton, *The Life of Captain Sir Richard F. Burton*, 2 vol. (1893, reprinted 1977); Thomas Wright, *The Life of Sir Richard Burton*, 2 vol. (1906, reprinted 1968), largely hostile; and Georgiana Stisted, *The True Life of Capt. Sir Richard F. Burton* (1896, reissued 1985), a panegyric by Burton's niece. Among later treatments are Alan Moorehead, *The White Nile*, rev. ed. (1971, reissued 1983); Byron Farwell, *Burton* (1963, reissued 1988); Fawn M.

Brodie, *The Devil Drives: A Life of Sir Richard Burton* (1967, reprinted 1984); and Edward Rice, *Captain Sir Richard Francis Burton* (1990, reissued 2001). Alexander Maitland, *Speke and the Discovery of the Source of the Nile* (2010; reprint of *Speke*, originally published in 1971), is the only full-length biography of Burton's rival explorer John Speke. Tim Jeal, *Explorers of the Nile: The Triumph and Tragedy of a Great Victorian Adventure* (2011), champions restoring Speke to the position of prominence that his discovery warrants. Speke's partner Samuel White Baker is the subject of Dorothy Middleton, *Baker of the Nile* (1949); and Richard Hall, *Lovers on the Nile* (1980).

Stanley's story as told in his *The Autobiography of Sir Henry Morton Stanley*, ed. by Dorothy Stanley (1909), was closely adhered to by Frank Hird, *H.M. Stanley: The Authorized Life* (1935), and others. A newer approach was the penetrating Richard Hall, *Stanley: An Adventurer Explored* (1974), based on most of the extant manuscript collections pertaining to Stanley; and that approach was continued in Frank McLynn, *Stanley: The Making of an Explorer* (1989); and in John Bierman, *Dark Safari: The Life Behind the Legend of Henry Morton Stanley* (1990). An authoritative biography is Tim Jeal, *Stanley: The Impossible Life of Africa's Greatest Explorer* (2007).

Works on the life and career of Charles George Gordon include Anthony Nutting, *Gordon of Khartoum: Martyr and Misfit* (1966); John Marlowe, *Mission to Khartum: The Apotheosis of General Gordon* (1969); and Charles Chenevix Trench, *Charley Gordon: An Eminent Victorian Reassessed* (1978; also published as *The Road to Khartoum: A Life of General Charles Gordon*, 1979). Cecil Northcott, *Robert Moffat: Pioneer in Africa, 1817–1870* (1961), chronicles the life of the Scottish missionary.

Helen Rosenman (trans. and ed.), *An Account in Two Volumes of Two Voyages to the South Seas...*, 2 vol. (1987), is a translation of selections from Jules-Sébastien-César Dumont d'Urville's earlier works. Biographies on explorers in Australia include E.M. Webster, *Whirlwinds in the Plain* (1980), on Ludwig Leichhardt; J.H.L. Cumpston, *Thomas Mitchell, Surveyor General & Explorer* (1955); and Gregory C. Eccleston, *Major Mitchell's 1836 "Australia Felix" Expedition: A Re-evaluation* (1992). George Seaver, *Francis Younghusband, Explorer and Mystic* (1952), is a biography, and Younghusband's expedition to Tibet is analyzed in Peter Fleming, *Bayonets to Lhasa* (1961, reprinted 1974); and Parshotam Mehra, *The Younghusband Expedition (To Lhasa): An Interpretation*, 2nd ed. (2005).

INDEX